Hoi
your Swiss German survival guide

Hoi

your Swiss German survival guide

Published 2005 and reprinted 2009 by
Bergli Books   Tel.: +41 61 373 27 77
Rümelinsplatz 19   Fax: +41 61 373 27 78
CH-4001 Basel   e-mail: info@bergli.ch
Switzerland   www.bergli.ch

ISBN 978-3-905252-13-2

Hoi
your Swiss German survival guide

Written by
Nicole Egger & Sergio J. Lievano

Illustrated & Designed by
Sergio J. Lievano

books

Contents

Preface	**vii**
Part I: About Swiss German	**3**
Introduction to Swiss German	4
Brief History of the Dialects	6
Use of High German in Switzerland	8
Difference Between Swiss and High German	9
Use of Swiss German	12
Part II: Survival Kit	**17**
Phonetics	18
Consonants	18
Vowels	19
Greetings & Socializing	20
Introduction	20
Understanding the Language	22
Questions	24
Small Talk	25
Invitations	28
Love	29
Things to Say at Special Moments	33
Work	34
Communication	38
Telephone	38
E-mail and SMS	40
Post Office	42
Media (News)	44
Food and Drinks	46
Health & Safety	54
Health	54
Human Body	58
Emotions	61
Emergency	64
Police	65
Shopping	68
Shopping in General	68
Clothes	70
Money & Banking	72

Traveling   74
    Transportation   74
    Directions   77
    Hotel   80
    Outdoors   82
    Entertainment   86
People   90
    Family   90
    Age   93
Housing   94
    Home   94
    Neighbours & Agencies   98
Miscellaneous   102
    Numbers   102
    Toilets   104
    General Non-Specific Terms   106
    Colours   107
    Animals   108
    Time   110
    Weather & Temperature   114

Part III: Decoding the Swiss   **117**
    Swiss Slanguage   118
    Swiss Idioms   122

Appendix   **127**
    Pronouns and Articles   128
    Verbs   130

The Dictionary   **133**
    English to Swiss German   134
    Swiss German to English   142

Index   **151**

About the Authors   **154**

Acknowledgements   **156**

Preface

If you want to feel at home in the German-speaking part of Switzerland, nothing will speed this process more than becoming acquainted with Swiss German. This book provides valuable tools, both for newcomers and for people who have been struggling with this language for a long time.

Swiss German is not one language, but the name given to the group of Alemannic dialects spoken within Switzerland. These dialects (their vocabulary, intonation and pronunciation) vary considerably from one neighbourhood to another. It is a spoken language, and there are contradictory spelling systems for the few occasions when it is written. **Hoi – your Swiss German survival guide** is based primarily on the dialect spoken in the Zurich area, which is spoken by more Swiss than the Swiss dialects spoken in Basel, Berne, Lucerne and other areas. Although the dialects vary in pronunciation and vocabulary, the Swiss usually understand dialects other than their own. This book will help you to do that, too.

Even though Swiss German is not written or standardized and has so many varieties, speakers of Swiss German from all levels of society are proud to speak it. Sharing a language that has so many variations keeps Swiss hearts and souls united.

Part I

About Swiss German

Introduction to Swiss German

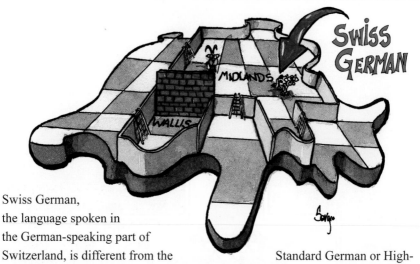

Swiss German,
the language spoken in
the German-speaking part of
Switzerland, is different from the   Standard German or High-
German spoken in Germany. The varieties of Swiss German dialect in Switzerland
cannot be defined so easily. No particular dialect is considered better than others.
Speaking dialect is not considered 'uneducated' or 'substandard' compared to

the written High
German but is spoken
proudly. A Swiss can
identify where another
Swiss grew up simply
from the dialect
spoken. For a Swiss
German speaker,
language is much
more than a way of
communication; it is
an integral part of his/
her national, regional and
even personal identity.

It is said that each
Swiss valley has its own dialect. This is
not an exaggeration. Mountains and other geographical
barriers have enabled some dialects to develop and
keep unique expressions. Some dialects,
such as the ones spoken in the Swiss
Midlands, have intermingled. The
interaction of speakers of different
dialects has made the peculiarities
of some dialects less prevalent.
The increasing mobility of the Swiss
accelerates this process and leads to
an increasingly neutral

"DIALÄKTGMISCH"

- a mixture of different
dialects.

5

Brief History of the Dialects

Although Switzerland is considered a
multilingual country, it did not start like that. Back in
1291 when Switzerland was created, the people founding
it all spoke a dialect of **Alemannic,** a branch of **Upper German**
covering what is now the south of Germany, Switzerland and Austria.

Alemannic tribes settled in Switzerland after the fall of the Roman Empire in the
5th century. These tribes settled predominantly along the Rhine and in the central
and north-eastern regions. Alemannic evolved from this time into three major
groups: 'Low', 'High' and 'Highest' Alemannic. These are not qualitative terms in
any way. These are the geographical terms describing where the dialect is spoken.
The 'Low', located in the Basel area; the 'High', in the vast majority of regions in
Switzerland, and the 'Highest' Alemannic, found in the remote area of the Wallis.

At the beginning of the 20th century, linguists thought Swiss German would
disappear by the end of the century and that the standard High German of Germany
would prevail in the German-speaking part of Switzerland.

However, the radical political events during this time and the growth of nationalism helped the Swiss retain their dialect as a form of national identity. During the 1930s the Swiss felt the need to distinguish themselves from the Germans, and speaking in Swiss dialect was a way of expressing Swiss patriotism.

Swiss German has reached a new level of acceptance, and continues to gain recognition and popularity, especially among the young, who like hearing it in Swiss popular music and who even compose written forms of it in their e-mail and SMS messages.

There have been many efforts to agree upon a consolidation of the main dialects into a standard Swiss German that could be written. Some rules exist, but the Swiss enjoy their diversity too much to agree on a unified Swiss German. Nevertheless, the use and popularity of Swiss German is steadily increasing in Switzerland.

The Swiss German Code

Although it is not well documented, it has been said on many occasions that throughout history, Swiss German dialects were sometimes used as a 'secret coding system' by people and institutions dealing directly or indirectly in political affairs.

Use of High German in Switzerland

Switzerland has what is defined as a 'Diglossia': a situation in a society where two languages are used which are closely related and functionally complementary. In the Swiss case, Swiss German is the spoken language, and High German, as the Swiss term 'Schriftdeutsch' defines it, is the official written language. High German is widely used in the written and spoken media, at schools, and also in the official, social, political or religious events where French-speaking Swiss, Italian-speaking Swiss and other non Swiss-German speakers might be present. Swiss German, on the other hand, is spoken in everyday, informal situations while shopping or socializing with friends and family, in local and regional radio and TV programs, in kindergartens, local government and non-government institutions.

Having Diglossia sometimes makes it difficult to know which language is most appropriate to speak – High German or the dialect. Since High German is their second language, Swiss German speakers are often reluctant to speak High German which does not always make it easy for them to communicate.

Difference between Swiss and High German

Swiss German has 'throaty' or guttural **'ch'** and **'k'** sounds. The intonation of Swiss German gives emphasis to the first syllable and pitch is more melodious than High German.

Swiss German speakers like to make every possible noun diminutive by placing the ending **'–li'** on it; for example, Gipfeli (croissant), Brötli (bread roll), Schäzzli (sweetheart), Chäzzli (little cat), etc.

Swiss German is also very receptive to the influences of foreign languages, in particular to English and French. Due to its geographical and cultural proximity to France, Swiss German has acquired a lot of French vocabulary, as opposed to how foreign words are 'Germanized' in Germany or Austria. The following table shows some examples of French influences on Swiss German:

Swiss German *(parenthesis shows pronounciation)*	High German	English
Merci *(Märsi)*	Danke	thank you
s Velo *(Welo)*	das Fahrrad	bicycle
dä Coiffeur *(Guafför)*	der Frisör	hairdresser
s Poulet *(Pule)*	das Hähnchen	chicken
s Cheminée *(Schmine)*	der Kamin	fireplace
s Spital *(Schpital)*	das Krankenhaus	hospital
dä Kondukteur *(Kondiktör)*	der Schaffner	train conductor
s Lavabo *(Lawabo)*	das Waschbecken	sink
dä Dessert *(Dessär)*	der Nachtisch	dessert
d' Saison *(Säson)*	die Jahreszeit	season

The four High German cases of nominative, accusative, dative and genitive are reduced in Swiss German to only two: the 'common case', which covers the German accusative and the nominative; and the 'dative case', which does likewise for the dative and the genitive. (See the Pronouns and Articles Section in the Appendix)

There are also certain misconceptions about Swiss German, due mainly to the fact that it is a spoken rather than a written language. Some people claim an absence of tenses, a lack of gender and of articles. Swiss German does, most certainly, have its own particular tenses (see the Verbs Section in the Appendix), it usually has the same genders as in High German, and it uses articles, even though these, as in most spoken languages, are abbreviated at a conversational level (see table on previous page).

The main differences between Swiss German and High German are related to vocabulary and pronunciation (intonation). Swiss dialects keep their unique, special terms and usually keep the original pronunciation of foreign words that are always creeping into the language.

German sentence construction

Translation: Hey! Someone stole your bike!

Use of Swiss German

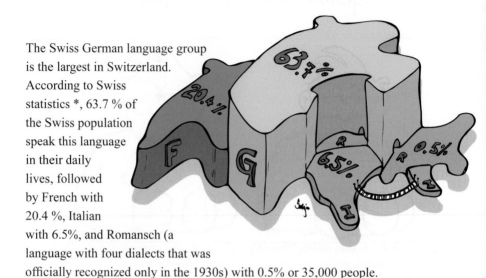

The Swiss German language group is the largest in Switzerland. According to Swiss statistics *, 63.7 % of the Swiss population speak this language in their daily lives, followed by French with 20.4 %, Italian with 6.5%, and Romansch (a language with four dialects that was officially recognized only in the 1930s) with 0.5% or 35,000 people.

The diversity of languages and their uneven distribution generate political and social discussions. The 'Röschtigraben' (fried–potato trench) is the name given to the ideological and linguistic border between the Swiss German and the French speaking area. It is not that there is any real conflict on this imaginary border. The relationship between neighbours is cordial and there is no hate or bitterness (other than the occasional reciprocal jokes). The Röschtigraben term – a kind of potato tortilla that originated in the German speaking part of Switzerland – denotes a different mind set between the two language groups, which is usually highlighted in the political arena.

The Swiss spare no effort to smooth out differences whenever possible, and equalize distribution of power and influence. The federalist form of government helps people living in Switzerland to maintain and respect regional and local distinctions.

* from press release 0351-0213-10 of the Swiss Federal Statistical Office, December 19, 2002.

The table on this page shows the multilingual environment where Swiss German is thriving. The large number of non-Swiss, who account for nearly one fifth of the Swiss population, plays an important role in the development of Swiss German. New Swiss generations come not only from Swiss families, but from a mixture of different nationalities and cultural backgrounds. These children

Other languages are*:	
Spanish	1.1 %
Serbian and Croatian	1.4 %
Portuguese	1.2 %
Turkish	0.6 %
English	1.0 %
Albanian	1.3 %
Other languages	2.4 %

of immigrants are called 'Secondos'. They may have little or no identity with their parents' original country and yet not be considered Swiss either.

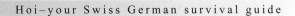

The 'Secondos' – a term that implies the second generation – act as a bridge of communication between their older relatives and Swiss people and add many new flavours to Swiss German.

Young Swiss are influenced by foreign music, foreign fashion, travel and the media, and are always adding new expressions to Swiss German. Like in other countries, Swiss youngsters create their own language identities, separating themselves from older generations.

Translation: Poor devil! No one told him about Swiss German...

Part II:

Survival Kit

Consonants

BE AWARE! Since Swiss German is mainly an oral language, this book will keep spelling rules as simple as possible. Therefore we do not use typical German spelling conventions such as **ck, tz, ieh, ah, oh,** etc. The only ones we kept are the v, that has the same pronunciation as f, and dt which is pronounced as t. Instead of **ck**, we used **kk**, for **tz** we used **zz** if the preceding vowel is short.

Tip Read the Swiss German words out loud as you go through this book. A Swiss Geman speaker also has to do this since the dialect is usually not written.

..ch..

Consonant Phonetics

b	as in **B**lues
ch	as in Lo**ch** Ness or Ba**ch**, always voiceless at the back of the throat
d	as in **D**oor
dt	't' as in Le**t**
f	as in **F**inger
g	as in **G**od
gg	short strong g (gk) as in French Ja**cqu**es
h	as in **H**ip-**H**op
j	as in **Y**es
k	throat rasping **Kh**
l	as in **L**ion
m	as in **M**e
n	as in **N**ight
ng	as in English Si**ng**

nk	ngk as in Thi**nk**
o	as in **O**lympics
p	as in **P**izza (never aspirated)
qu	as in **Qu**antity
r	as in Bu**rr**ito (usually rolled like in Spanish)
s	as in **S**ad (voiceless)
t	as in French **T**u (rather soft, never aspirated)
v	'f' as in **F**inger
w	'v' as in **V**alentine
x	'gs' as in Me**x**ico
z	'ts' as in Lo**ts**

Double consonants are preceded by a short vowel.

Vowels

Vowel Phonetics

a	as in **A**frica	**ö**	as in French D**eux**
ä	as in **Bea**r	**u**	as in C**oo**l / M**oo**n
ai	as in **Eye**	**ü**	as in French T**u**
au	as in H**ow**	**y**	as in French T**u** (except
e	as in **E**lephant		for English words)
ei	as in H**ey**		
i	as in **Ea**sy	**Double vowels** double the
o	as in **O**racle	length of the sound.

WARNING! Swiss phonetics are one of the most complex subjects to discuss. As mentioned in the first part of the book, there are no standard rules and the sounds of letters and words vary from one area to the other. This book gives an approximation of the standard way Swiss German is pronounced in the Zurich region.

LEDÄLÄ ?
LEDELE ?
LADELÄ ?
LÄDÄLE ?

BE AWARE! To help you understand Swiss pronunciation of foreign words, a phonetic pronunciation is given in parenthesis.

* LÄDÄLÄ : TO GO SHOPPING

Introduction

Formal and Informal

Swiss German differentiates between the formal and the informal way of approaching a person. The formal way uses the pronoun **'Sii'** and the person is usually addressed by his / her last name ('Good morning Mr. Meier), the informal way is used with the pronoun **'du'** and the person can be addressed by his/ her first name ('Hi Chris...').

Saying Hello (Formal)

Good morning Mr. / Mrs.	Guätä Morgä Herr / Frau...
	Guätä Tag
Good afternoon.	Guätä Namittag.
Good evening.	Guätä n'Aabig.
Hello.	Grüezi.
Hello. (to several people)	Grüezi mitenand.
How are you?	Wiä gat's Inä?
Fine, and you?	Guät, und Inä?
Pleased to meet you.	Froit mich, Sii kännä z'lärnä.
'Bye.	Uf widerluägä.
	Uf widersee.
	Adieu (Adjö)

Formal (Sii)

To be used in business, with strangers, with seniors, or whenever you meet a grown-up that hasn't introduced him / herself with his / her first name. Usually the older, more senior, person offers the **'du'** form **(Sii chönd du zu mir sägä)** or **'wämmer Duzis machä?'**

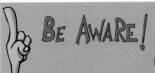

In this book the abbreviation **(inf)** is used for **informal** and **(fr)** is used for **formal**. For nouns: **(m)** is **masculine**, **(f)** is **feminine**, **(n)** is **neutral** and **(pl)** is **plural**.

Saying Hello (Informal)

Hi.	Hoi. / Sali. / Salü.
Hi. (to several people)	Hoi zäme.
How are you?	Wiä gat's? Wiä häsch äs?
Fine, and you?	Guät, und dir?
Quite OK.	Scho rächt.
I am not so well.	Mir gat's nöd so guät.
'Bye.	Ciao. *(tschau)* / Tschüss.
See you.	Mer gseet sich!
Pleased to meet you.	Froit mich, di kännä z'lärnä.
See you later.	Bis schpöter.
Have a nice day / evening.	No än schönä Tag. / Aabig.

Informal: (du / ier)

Usually used with children, friends, family, and among students and colleagues.

21

Understanding the Language

Key Survival Phrases

Do you speak English?	Chönd Sii Änglisch? (fr)
	Chasch Änglisch? (inf)
Sorry, I don't understand.	Sorry, ich verschtaa Sii nöd. (fr)
	Sorry, ich verschtaa di nöd. (inf)
What did you say?	Was händ Sii gsait? (fr)
	Was häsch gsait? (inf)
Can you repeat what you said?	Chönd Sii bitte widerholä, was Sii gsait händ? (fr)
	Chasch nomal sägä, was gsait häsch? (inf)
Could you write it down?	Chönted Sii mir das ufschriibä? (fr)
	Chasch mir das ufschriibä? (inf)
Can you say it again slowly?	Chönd Sii das nomal langsam sägä? (fr)
	Chasch das nomal langsam sägä? (inf)
I don't speak Swiss German.	Ich cha kai Schwiizerdütsch.

Chönä is used for both ability and politeness (are you able to? / could you?). In the formal question, the form is '**Chönd Sii?**'; the informal question is '**Chasch?**'. For verb conjugation in Swiss German, check the tables in the Appendix at the end of the book.

Greetings & Socializing

 **WARNING!**

Being Polite

In Switzerland (as in many other countries) a golden rule for good communication and understanding is to be polite. Therefore the following words may be very useful when meeting people:

Please.	Bitte.
Thank you.	Danke. / Merci. *(märsi)*
Thanks a lot.	Danke villmal.
Excuse me.	Entschuldigung. / Exgüsi.
May I?	Chönt ich?
	Törf ich?
Yes, please.	Ja, bitte.
No, thank you.	Nai, danke.
I am sorry.	(Äs) tuät mir Laid.
You are welcome.	Bitte, gärn gschee.
You are very kind.	Sii sind seer nätt. (fr)
	Sii sind seer hilfsberait. (fr)
	Du bisch seer nätt. (inf)
	Du bisch seer hilfsberait. (inf)
Would you mind…?	Chönted Sii bitte…? (fr)
	Chöntisch bitte…? (inf)

23

Greetings & Socializing

Questions

 There are two types of questions:

1. For open questions, where the potential answers are unlimited, the question always starts with a question word (also called w-word) **Wo woonsch?** (Where do you live?), **Was isch dini Liäblingsmusig?** (What's your favourite music?)
2. For closed questions, where the answer is either yes or no, there is no special question word. The question starts with a verb and then the subject: **Chasch (du) Dütsch?** (Do you speak German?) **Schaffsch (du) in Züri?** (Do you work in Zürich?)

Why?
Warum?

When?
Wänn?

What ?
Was ?

How?
Wiä?

Where?
Wo?

How many?
Wiä vill ?

How long?
Wiä lang?

Who?
Wär?

To where.?
Wohi? / woannä ?

From where?
Vo wo?

How much?
Wiä vill?

Who with?
Mit wäm?

What for?
Warum?/ Für was?

Small Talk

Introducing Yourself

What is your name?	Wiä isch Irä Namä? (fr)
	Wiä haissed Sii? (fr)
	Wiä isch din Namä? (inf)
	Wiä haissisch? (inf)
My name is...	Ich haissä...
Where are you from?	Wohär chömed Sii? (fr)
	Wohär chunnsch du? (inf)
I come from...	Ich chumä us...
Where do you live?	Wo woned Sii? (fr)
	Wo wonsch? (inf)
I live in...	Ich wonä in...
How long have you been here?	Wiä lang sind Sii scho da? (fr)
	Wiä lang bisch scho da? (inf)
I have been here for...years.	Ich bi scho....Jaar da.
What do you do in your spare time?	Was mached Sii i Irerä Freiziit? (fr)
	Was machsch i dinerä Freiziit? (inf)
I like...	Ich ha... gärn
I love...	Ich liäbä...
I'm interested in...	Ich interessierä mich für...

Tip Swiss German is a so-called 'pro drop' language, which means the subject can be left out, but only in the first and second person singular. One can say: **Ich chumä**, or just **chumä** (the second being more colloquial).

25

Greetings & Socializing

The Swiss German word **'ledig'**
means 'Not married'. The English
word **'single'** is also used in Swiss
German, but it only means 'with no boyfriend / girlfriend'
(not in a relationship). So one can be **'ledig'** but not **'single'**,
meaning one lives with somebody without being married.

Getting **Personal**

Are you married?	Sind Sii ghürätä? (fr)
	Sind Sii verhüratet? (fr)
	Bisch ghürätä? (inf)
	Bisch verhüratet? (inf)
Are you single?	Sind Sii single? (fr)
	Bisch single? (inf)
Do you have a boy / girlfriend?	Händ Sii än Fründ / ä Fründin? (fr)
	Häsch än Fründ / ä Fründin? (inf)
Do you have children?	Händ Sii Chind? (fr)
	Häsch Chind? (inf)
How is your family?	Wiä gat's Irerä Familiä? (fr)
	Wiä gat's dinerä Familiä? (inf)
What's your telephone number?	Wiä isch Iri Telefonnummerä? (fr)
	Wiä isch dini Telefonnummerä?(inf)
My number is…	Mini Nummerä isch…
I don't have an e-mail address.	Ich ha kai Emailadrässä.
What's your address?	Wiä isch Iri Adrässä? (fr)
	Wiä isch dini Adrässä? (inf)
Which street?	A wellärä Schtrass?

First Approach

Do you want to go and have a drink?	Wänd Sii ais go ziä? (fr)
	Wänd Sii öppis go trinkä? (fr)
	Wotsch ais go ziä? (inf)
	Wotsch öppis go trinkä? (inf)
Can I invite you for a drink?	Chann ich Inä än Drink schpendierä? (fr)
	Chann ich dir än Drink schpendierä? (inf)
Do you want to come with me / us ?	Chunnsch mit mir / ois?
Are you coming?	Chömed Sii? (fr) / Chunnsch? (inf)
Let's go somewhere.	Gömmer noimät anä.
Do I know you from somewhere?	Känn ich Sii vo noimät?(fr) / Känned mir ois?
	Känn ich di vo noimät? (inf)
Do you want to dance?	Wänd Sii tanzä?(fr)
	Wotsch tanzä? (inf)
Do you have a cigarette?	Händ Sii ä Zigarettä? (fr)
	Häsch ä Zigi? (inf)

Negative Answers

No, I don't smoke.	Nai, ich rauchä nöd.
I have to go now.	Ich muäs jezt gaa.
Please, leave me alone!	Lönd Sii mich bitte in Ruä! (fr)
	La mich bitte in Ruä! (inf)
Get lost!	Hau ab! (inf) / Haued Sii ab! (fr)
I don't think so.	Ich glaub nöd.
I want to go home.	Ich möcht hai.
I need to go home.	Ich muäs hai.
I have to work tomorrow.	Ich muäs morn schaffä.
I have no time.	Ich ha kai Ziit.
I don't have any money.	Ich ha kai Gäld.
I don't feel like.	Ich ha kai Luscht.

Invitations

Key Survival Phrases

May I invite you for dinner tomorrow night?
Törf ich Sii morn aabig zum Ässä iiladä?(fr)
Törf ich di morn aabig zum Ässä iiladä? (inf)

Yes, I would love to come. Ja, ich chumä gärn.

Thank you for the invitation. Danke für d'Iiladig.

to be on time pünktlich sii

to be late verschpötet sii

Sorry for being late. Entschuldigung für d'Verschpötig.

The food is delicious. S'Ässä isch seer fain / s'Ässä schmökkt wunderbar.

Please bring your partner. Sii chönd gärn Irä Partner / Iri Partnerin mitbringä. (fr)
Du chasch gärn din Fründ / dini Fründin mitnää. (inf)

No, I am sorry, but I have another appointment.
Tuät mir Laid, da chani nöd. Ich ha dänn scho öppis vor.

Tip In Switzerland, people usually bring something to a party. The most common gifts are wine, sweets or flowers. When invited to a barbecue or an informal party, it is polite to offer to bring something: **Chann ich öppis mitbringä?** (Can I bring something?)

Common Swiss Events

Party	Party (f) *(Parti)*
	Fäscht (n)
Birthday party	Geburtstags-party (f)
Barbecue	Grillfäscht (n)
Farewell party	Apschidsfäscht (n)
Brunch	Brunch (m)
Lunch	Zmittagässä (n)
Dinner	Znacht (m)
	Znachtässä (n)
Coffee party	Kafiklatsch (m)
	Kafichränzli (n)
Hen night / Stag night	Polteraabig (m)
Housewarming party	Husiweiigs-party (f)

Love

The Swiss are keen on pet names, the most common of which are:

Schäzzli (little treasure), **Tübli** (little dove), **Müüsli** (little mouse), **Chäferli** (little beetle), **Schnugi** (sweetie), **Bärli** (little bear).

Key Survival Phrases (informal)

to love	liäbä
I love you.	Ich liäbä di / Ich ha di gärn. *(see Tip p.30)*
I need you.	Ich bruchä di.
I miss you.	Ich vermissä di.
You are very pretty / sexy.	Du bisch mega / seer hübsch / sexy.
You are the love of my life.	Du bisch d'Liäbi vo mim Läbä.
Kiss me.	Küss mich.
I've fallen in love with you.	Ich ha mich i di verliäbt.
We fell in love.	Mir händ ois verliäbt.
I am in love.	Ich bi verliäbt.
Let's move in / live together.	Chumm mir ziänd zäme.
You make me very happy.	Du machsch mich total / mega happy.
She is my girlfriend.	Sii isch mini Fründin.
He is my boyfriend.	Er isch min Fründ.
We are just friends.	Mir sind nur Kollegä.
We love each other.	Mir liäbed ois.
I like her / him.	Er / Sii gfallt mir.
Love at first sight.	Liäbi uf dä erschti Blikk.
We first met in...	Mit händ ois in…kän glärnt.
Partner	Partner (m) / Partnerin (f)
	Läbäspartner (m) / Läbäspartnerin (f)
to get to know each other	sich kännä lernä

Greetings & Socializing

BE AWARE! In Swiss German, the words **'Fründ (m)'** and **'Fründin (f)'** refer to a friend, as well as a boyfriend or girlfriend. When the Swiss want to make it clear that somebody is their boyfriend or girlfriend, they may say: **min Fründ** (my friend) for boyfriend or **mini Fründin** for girlfriend. **Än Fründ (m)** or **ä Fründin (f),** on the other hand, is just a friend. The word **'Kolleg'** is also used for friends, including friends outside work that aren't colleagues in the English sense.

'Ich ha di gärn' (I like you) may be understood romantically, but not necessarily. **'Ich liäbä di,'** (I love you) on the other hand, is strong and is mainly used in a romantic context and not between friends.

WARNING!

Many mistakes are made just by the wrong usage of the preposition that comes together with the verb. In order not to jeopardise good communication keep in mind the following:

bim John/ bi dä Anna schlafä
Sleep at John's / Anna's place

näbäd äm John/ näbäd dä Anna schlafä
Sleep next to John / Anna

mit äm John/ mit dä Anna schlafä
Sleep with John/ Anna (to have sex).

Sexual Preferences	
I like women.	Ich schtaa uf Frauä.
I like men.	Ich schtaa uf Manä.
heterosexual	hetero(sexuell)
homosexual	homo(sexuell)
gay	schwul
lesbian	lesbisch

Wedding **Stuff**

to get engaged	sich verlobä *
I got engaged.	Ich ha mich verlobt.
to get married	hüratä
to be married	ghüratä sii
I am married.	Ich bi ghüratä.
Marriage	Ehe (f)
Wedding	Hochziit (f)
We are getting married.	Mir hüratet.
Wedding eve's party	Polteraabig (m)
Do you want to marry me?	Möchtisch mich hüratä? (inf)
	Möchtisch mini Frau / min Maa werdä? (inf)
Yes, I do.	Ja, ich will.
No, I don't want to / yet.	Nai, ich möcht nöd / nonig.

EXCUSE ME...
CAN YOU TAKE A PHOTO
OF US ?

GRAMMAR

* **Sich verlobä / sich verliäbä** are reflexive verbs. Reflexive verbs have the following conjugation:

ich verliäbä *mich*
du verliäbsch *di*
er/sii verliäbt *sich*
mir verliäbed *ois*
ier verliäbed *oi*
sii verliäbed *sich*

Greetings & Socializing

Loveless (informal)

I don't want to see you again.	Ich möcht di niä wider gsee.
There is someone else.	Ich ha än anderä (m) / än anderi. (f)
I hate you.	Ich hassä di.
Let's take a break.	Chumm, mir mached ä Pausä.
Have you been unfaithful?	Häsch du mich betrogä?
We are just friends.	Mir sind nur Kollegä.
I am not in love.	Ich bi nöd verliäbt.
to move out	uusziä
S/he moved out.	Sii/Er isch uszogä.
to have an affair	än Affärä ha
to betray somebody	öpper betrügä
S/he betrayed me.	Sii/Er hätt mich betrogä.
Argument	Schtriit (m)
argue	schtriitä
to separate	sich tränä
to get a divorce	sich schaidä la
divorced	gschidä
to hate each other	sich hassä

GRAMMAR

Sich schaidä la is an expression that is used in the following way:

Ich la mich schaidä.
(I am getting a divorce)
Ich will mich schaidä la.
(I want to get a divorce)
Sii lönd sich schaidä.
(They are getting a divorce)

SLAM!

Things to Say at Special Moments

Survival Words and Phrases

Happy Birthday!	Alles Gueti zum Geburtstag!
Merry Christmas!	Schöni Wiänachtä!
Happy New Year!	Äs guäts Nois! / Än guätä Rutsch!
	Äs guäts nois Jaar!
I wish you…	Ich wünschä dir (inf) / Inä (fr)…
Happy Anniversary!	Än guetä Jaarestag! Ä schöns Jubiläum!
Good Luck!	Vill Glükk! / Vill Erfolg!
Best wishes!	Alles Gueti!
Fantastic!	Fantastisch!
Beautiful!	Schön!
Delicious!	So fain!
Welcome!	Willkomä!
Break a leg!	Hals und Baibruch!
Enjoy your meal!	Än Guetä!
Congratulations!	Alles Gueti!
	Ich gratulierä
To your health!	Uf dini Gsundhait!
I wish you success!	Vill Erfolg!
Have a nice trip!	Schöni Rais!
Get well!	Gueti Besserig!
Cheers!	Proscht! / Pröschtli!

Misfortune and Sympathy

Sorry.	Äs tuät mir Laid. / Sorry.
My deepest condolences.	Mis tüfi Biilaid.
I hope you get well soon.	Ich hoffä, äs gat bald besser.
Bad luck	Päch
Better luck next time.	Vill Glükk snächscht Mal.
What a shame!	Schad!
I warned you.	Ich ha di gwarnt.

33

Work

Key Survival Phrases

Do you work?	Sind Sii pruäfstätig? / Schaffed Sii? (fr)
	Bisch pruäfstätig? / Schaffsch? (inf)
What do you do?	Was mached Sii? / Was schaffed Sii?(fr)
	Was machsch? / Was schaffsch? (inf)
What is your profession?	Was isch Irä Pruäf ? (fr)
	Was händ Sii glärnt? (fr)
	Was isch din Pruäf ? (inf)
	Was häsch glärnt? (inf)
I am...	Ich bi...
Where do you work?	Wo schaffed Sii? (fr)
	Wo schaffsch? (inf)
I work at...	Ich schaffä bi...
I work at home.	Ich schaffä dähai.
I work freelance.	Ich bin unäbhängig.
I am not working.	Ich schaffä nöd.
I am employed at...	Ich bin agschtellt bi...
I am unemployed.	Ich bin arbetslos.
I am self-employed.	Ich bi sälbscht-schtändig.

Continued on the next page...

Appraisal	Quali(fikation) (f)	**Minutes**	Protokoll (n)
	Laischtigsbewärtig (f)	**Invoice**	Rächnig (f)
Contract	Vertrag (m)	**Purchase order**	Pschtellig (f)
Form	Formular (n)		Uuftrag (m)
Job application	Bewärbig (f)		
Plan	Plan (m)		
Report	Pricht (m)		

Paperwork

The working environment in Switzerland is probably the most common place where English and Swiss German merge. English remains as the international business language, so the business area names tend to be in English (e.g. **Customer Service**, **Finance**, **Procurement**, **Supply Chain…**).

Work

Key Survival Phrases

have a meeting	Ich hann äs Meeting / ä Sizzig / ä Beschprächig.
We have a problem.	Mir händ äs Problem.
We are successful.	Mir sind seer erfolgriich.
We made … profit.	Mir händ … Gwünn gmacht.
We made … turnover.	Mir händ… Umsazz gmacht.
We made… loss.	Mir händ … Verluscht gmacht.
We create jobs.	Mir schaffed Arbetspläzz.
You have the job.	Sii händ d'Schtell.
You are fired.	Sii sind entlaa.
I want to resign.	Ich möcht kündigä.
I want a salary raise.	Ich möcht ä Loonerhöig.
Would you have lunch with me?	Chömed Sii mit mir go zmittagässä? (fr)
	Chunnsch mit mir go zmittagässä? (inf)
Could you explain please?	Chönd Sii mir das bitte erchlärä? (fr)
	Chasch mir das erchlärä? (inf)
I want to go on holiday from …till…	Ich möcht vo….bis…. i d'Feriä.
Could you make a presentation for me?	Chönd Sii mir ä Präsentazion machä? (fr)
	Chasch mir ä Präsentazion machä? (inf)
I would like to discuss something with you.	Ich möcht öppis mit Inä beschprächä. (fr)
	Ich möcht öppis mit dir beschprächä. (inf)

Work

Payment

Payment	Zalig (f)
Bonus	Bonus (m)
Salary	Loon (m)
	Salär (n)
Fee	Gebür (f)
	Priis (m)
Overtime	Überschtundä (pl)
Commission	Komission (f)
Costs	Choschtä (pl)
Pension fund	Pensionskassä (f)
Discounts	Verbilligung (f)
Insurance	Versicherig (f)
Taxes	Schtürä (pl)
Part time	tailziit
Full time	vollziit

Time @ Work

Appointment	Termin (m)
Break	Pausä (f)
Coffee break	Kafipausä (f)
Conference	Konfäränz (f)
Job interview	Bewärbigsgschpräch (n)
Vacations	Feriä (pl)
Presentation	Präsentazion (f)
Course	Kurs (m)
Lunch break	Mittagspausä (f)
Meeting	Beschprächig (f)
	Sizzig (f)
	Meeting (n) *(miiting)*

Working Areas

Smoking area	Rauchereggä (m)
Office	Gschäft (n)
	Büro (n)
Canteen	Kantinä (f)
	Mensa (f)
Warehouse	Lagerhallä (f)
	Warähuus (n)
Reception	Empfang (m)
Studio	Schtudio (n)
Garage	Garage (f) *(Garasch)*
Parking area	Parkplazz (m)
Laboratory	Labor (n)

Dress Code

Dress Code	Chlaidervorschrift (f)	Tie	Grawattä (f)
Business casual	unzwungä	Uniform	Uniform (f)
Suit	Aazug (m)	Briefcase	Arbetsmappä (f)
		Dress	Chlaid (n)

Work

Job Title

Board of Directors	Verwaltigsrat (m)	**Worker**	Arbaiterin (f)
Boss	Chef (m) *(Schef)*	**Trainee**	Praktikant (m)
	Chefin (f) *(Schefin)*		Praktikantin (f)
Employer	Arbetgeber (m)	**Customer**	Chund (m)
	Arbetgeberin (f)		Chundin (f)
Employee	Agschtellte (m)	**Occupation**	Job (m) *(Tschop)*
	Agschtellti (f)		Pruäf (m)
Colleague	Arbetskolleg (m)	**Job description**	Jobbeschribig (f)
	Arbetskollegin (f)	**Secretary**	Sekretär/in (m/f)
Director	Diräktor (m)		Sekretär (m)
	Diräktorin (f)	**Assistant**	Asischtänt (m)
Manager	Manager (m) *(Mänätscher)*		Asischtäntin (f)
	Managerin(f)*(Mänätscherin)*	**Technician**	Techniker (m)
Partner	Partner (m)		Technikerin (f)
	Partnerin (f)	**Consultant**	Berater (m)
Professional	Profi (m)		Beraterin (f)
Owner	Psizzer (m)	**Cleaner**	Puzzma (m)
	Psizzerin (f)		Puzzfrau (f)
Salesperson	Verchoiffer (m)	**Receptionist**	Resepzionischt (m)
Salesperson	Verchoifferin (f)		Resepzionischtin (f)
Worker	Arbaiter (m)	**Apprentice**	Leerling (m)

Telephone

Communication

When Calling

May I talk to Mr. X / Ms. Y?	Chann ich mit äm Herr X / dä Frau Y redä? (fr)
Could you connect me to Mr. X?	Chönted Sii mich bitte mit äm Härr X verbindä? (fr)
I'll connect you.	Ich verbindä Sii
Can I call you back?	Chann ich Inä zrugglütä? (fr)
	Chann ich dir zrugglütä? (inf)
What are you calling about...?	Um was gat's?

...YOUR CALL IS BEING HELD IN A QUEUE. THE WAITING TIME IS CURRENTLY 25 MINUTES. IN THE MEANTIME, LET US INTRODUCE YOU TO OUR NEW PRODUCTS AND SERVICES THAT WILL ENSURE TOTAL CUSTOMER SATISFACTION...

Telephone Words

Answering machine	Telefonbeantworter (m)
Area code	Vorwaal (f)
cancel	löschä / känslä
Local call	lokalä Aaruäf (m)
Long distance call	internazionalä Aaruäf (m)
Mobile phone	Händi (n) / Natel (n)
Operator	Vermittlig (f)
Phone call	Aaruäf (m)
Public telephone	öffentlichs Telefon (n)
Telephone bill	Telefonrächnig (f)
Telephone book	Telefonbüach (n)
Telephone card	Telefonchartä (f)
to telephone / call	aalütä

When answering a phone call, Swiss usually say their full name: **Christa Müller.** When calling, Swiss usually introduce themselves: **Da isch d'Christa Müller. Chönt ich bitte mit äm Herr Meier redä?** (This is Christa Müller speaking. May I talk to Mr. Meier?). A phone conversation is usually ended with:

Uf Widerhörä.
It is also polite to ask **Stör ich?** (Am I disturbing you?), when calling somebody unexpectedly, or **Händ Sii churz Ziit?** (fr) (Do you have a moment?) at the beginning of a conversation.

Key Survival Phrases

Can I use your phone?	Chann ich mal Iräs Telefon benuzzä? (fr)
	Chann ich mal dis Telefon benuzzä? (inf)
I will call you.	Ich lüt Inä aa. (fr)
	Ich lüt dir aa. (inf)
There was no answer.	Niämärt hätt abgno.
The line is busy / engaged.	Äs isch psezt.
I want to make a collect call to...	Ich möcht äs R-Gschpröch nach ... machä.
I need to recharge my mobile phone.	Ich muäs mis Natel ufladä.
There is no telephone line.	Äs hätt kai Verbindig.
The phone is ringing.	S'Telefon lütet.
Wrong number.	Falsch verbundä.
How much does a minute cost to...?	Wiä vill choschtet's ä Minutä uf ... z'telefonierä?
Please turn off your mobile phone.	Schtelled Sii bitte Iräs Händi ab. (fr)
	Schtell bitte dis Händi ab. (inf)

Communication

E-mail and SMS

Communication

Warning: Your Password has not been recognised please try again...

E-mail

		Laptop	Laptop (m) *(Läptop)*
Symbol '@'	Affeschwanz (m)	log in	iiloggä
Address book	Addrässbuäch (n)	log out	uusloggä
Connection	Verbindig (f)	reply	antwortä
copy	kopierä		zruggschriibä
Desktop	Desktop (m)	Subject	Thema (n)
Attachment	Attachment (n)	Trash	Apfallchorb (m)
	(Attätschmänt)		Apfall (m)
forward	forwardä	E-mail	E-mail (n)
	wiiterlaitä		Mail (n) *(Meil)*
Text message	SMS (n) *(Äsämäs)*		

Key Computer Terms

Printer	Printer (m) / Drukker (m)
print	drukkä
Screen	Bildschirm (m)
open a program	Äs Programm öffnä
save a program	Äs Programm abschpaicherä
burn a CD	Ä CD bränä *(Zede)*
open a new folder	Än noiä Ordner aleggä
turn on the computer	Dä Computer aaschtelä
turn off the computer	Dä Computer usschaltä
Download	abeladä / downlowdä *(daunloudä)*

Survival E-mail Phrases

I need to check my e-mails.	Ich muäs mal mini Emails aaluägä.
There is no Internet connection.	Äs hätt kai Internetaaschluss.
That is a virus / spam.	Ich hann än Wirus / äs Späm-Mail.
I will e-mail you.	Ich schrib Inä äs Email. (fr)
	Ich maile dir. (inf)
Send me an e-mail.	Schribed Sii mir äs Email bitte. (fr)
	Schrib mer äs Mail. (inf)
I deleted your e-mail.	Ich ha Iräs Mail glöscht. (fr)
	Ich ha dis Mail glöscht. (inf)
Stop sending me e-mails.	Schribed Sii mir kai Mails me. (fr)
	Schrib mer kai Email me (inf)
What's your e-mail?	Was isch Iri Email? (fr)
	Was isch dini Email? (inf)

Communication

Swiss SMS terms

LG	Liäbi Grüess(li) (kind regards)
HDG	Ha di gärn (I like you)
GN8	Guät Nacht (Good night)
8UNG	Achtung (be careful / watch out)
CUL8r	See you later *
4U	For you *

* English terms are commonly used.

Post Office

Communication

The Post

Envelope	Couvert (n) *(Kuwäär)*	**Postcard**	Poschtchartä (f)
Address	Adrässä (f)	**Airmail**	Luftposcht (f)
Sender's address	Apsänder/in (m/f)	**Registered letter**	igschribnä Briäf (m)
Post office	Poscht (f)	**Registered mail**	igschribni Poscht (f)
Mail box	Briäfchaschtä (m)	**Postcode**	Poschtlaitzaal (f)
Postman	Pöschtler (m)	**to send**	sändä
	Pöschtlerin (f)		schikkä
Packet	Päkkli (n)	**Stamp**	Markä (f)
Letter	Briäf (m)	**Care of**	zuhandä vo
Postage stamp	Poschtschtämpfel (m)	**Postal money order**	Gäldüberwiisig (f)
Post	Poscht (f)		

Survival Post Phrases

I'd like to send this letter fast delivery.
Ich möcht dä Briäf mit A-Poscht schikkä.

I would like to redirect my post.
Ich möcht mini Poscht umlaitä.

What's the postcode of...?
Was isch d'Poschtlaitzaal vo...?

How much does it cost to send this package high priority?
Wiä vill choschtet's dä Briäf mit A-Poscht z'schikkä?

How can I apply for a P.O. Box?
Wiä chumm ich äs Poschtfach über?

What's the fastest way to send this letter / package?
Wiä chann ich dä Briäf / das Päkkli am schnellschtä schikkä?

What's the cheapest way to send this letter / package?
Wiä chann ich dä Briäf / das Päkkli am billigschtä schikkä?

When will it arrive?
Wänn chunnt's a?

Can you give me a price list?
Händ Sii mir ä Priislischtä?

Tip

The Swiss postal system offers different possibilities for sending letters and packages. The most common ones are:

B- Poscht: Low priority delivery. Within Switzerland it usually takes two to three days for letters to be delivered.
A- Poscht: High Priority delivery. Within Switzerland it usually takes one day for letters to be delivered.
Express: Fast Delivery.
Iigschriibä: Certified or recorded delivery. It requires a signature from the recipient.

website: www.swisspost.ch

Communication

43

Media (News)

In the News

		Gossip	Klatsch (m)
Advertising	Wärbig (f)		Tratsch (m)
Article	Artikel (m)	**to gossip**	klatschä
Art	Kunscht (f)	**Headlines**	Schlagzilä (pl)
Bulletin board	Aschlagbrätt (n)	**International news**	Ussland-Nachrichtä (pl)
Cable TV	Kabelfernse (n)	**Local news**	lokali Noiigkaitä (pl)
Celebrity	Promi (m)		lokali Nachrichtä (pl)
	VIP (m) *(Wiaipi)*	**Magazine**	Heftli (n)
Channel	Kanal (m)	**Music**	Musig (f)
Culture	Kultur (f)	**National news**	Inland-Nachrichtä (pl)
Editor	Herusgeber (m)		
	Herusgeberin (f)		
Famous	berüämt / bekannt		**Continued on the next page…**
Fashion	Modä (f)		

In the News

News	Nachrichtä (pl)
Newspaper	Zitig (f)
Obituary	Todesaazaig (f)
Opinion	Mainig (f)
Photo	Foti (n)
Radio	Radio (m)
Satellite	Satellit (m)
Section	Apschnitt (m)
	Tail (m)
Society	Gsellschaft (f)
Sports	Schport (m)
Talk show	Talk Show (f) *(Tok Schou)*
Television	Fernse (n)
Television licence	Fernsebewilligung (f)

Food & Drinks

Food & Drinks

Key Survival Phrases

I'm hungry.	Ich ha Hunger.
I'm thirsty.	Ich ha Turscht.
A table for two, please.	Än Tisch für zwai, bitte.
Can I see the menu, please?	Händ Sii mir ä Schpiis-chartä bitte? Chann ich emal d'Spiis-chartä aluägä, bitte?
I would like…	Ich möcht...
with / without spicy sauce	mit scharfer Sosä / ooni scharfi Sosä
with / without lemon	mit / ooni Zitrone
A little…	Äs bizzeli...
A bottle of mineral water, please.	Ä Fläschä Wasser, bitte
with / without ice…	Mit / ooni Iis
A beer, please / a wheat beer, please.	Ä Schtangä, bitte. / Äs Waizä, bitte.
Can I have the bill, please?	Chann ich zalä, bitte?
Can you split the bill?	Chömmer tränt zalä?
Did you enjoy the meal?	Isch guät gsi? / Isch rächt gsi?
The food was good / bad.	S'Ässä isch guät / nöd so guät gsi.
to take away	zum Mitnää

Meat

Meat	Flaisch (n)
Bacon	Schpäkk (m)
Beef	Rindflaisch (n)
Chicken	Huän (n)
	Poulet (n) *(Pule)*
Ham	Schinkä (m)
Lamb	Lamm (n)
Liver	Läbere (f)
Pork	Schwinigs (n)
	Schwaineflaisch (n)
Salami	Salami (m)
Sausage	Wurscht (f)
Steak	Steak (n) *(Steik)*
Turkey	Truthaan (m)
Veal	Chalbflaisch (n)

Meals

Meals	Maalzitä (pl)
Starter	Vorschpiis (f)
Appetizer	Aperitif (m)
Breakfast	Zmorgä (m)
Dessert	Dessert (m) *(Dessär)*
Dinner / Supper	Znacht (m)
Lunch	Zmittag (m)
Main course	Hauptschpiis (f)
Snack (morning)	Znüni (m)
Snack (afternoon)	Zvieri (m)

Food & Drinks

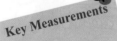

Key Measurements

Kilo	Kilo (n)
Litre	Liter (m)
Pound	Pfund (n)

Meat Preparation

rare	bluetig
medium	medium
	halb durä
well done	guät durä

Food & Drinks

Coffee & Hot Drinks

Cappuccino	Cappuccino (m) *(Gaputschino)*	**Punch**	Punsch (m)
		Hot chocolate	Haissi Schoggi (f)
Coffee (with cream)	Kafi (crème) (m)	**Hot milk**	Haissi Milch (f)
Coffee with milk	Milchkafi (m) Schalä (f)	**Latte Macchiato**	Latte Macchiato (f) *(Latte Maggiato)*
Expresso	Espresso (m)	**Tea**	Tee (m)

BE AWARE! The Swiss tend to call '**Tee**' any type of water infusion, so if you want a cup of black tea with milk it is better to specify: '**Schwarztee mit crème**' or just '**Tee crème**'.

Cold Drinks

Cold drinks	Chalti Getränk (pl)
Apple juice	Öpfelsaft (m) Süässmoscht (m)
Coke	Coggi (n)/ Cola (n)
Grapefruit juice	Grapefruitsaft (m) *(Gräpfrüsaft)*
Grape juice	Truubesaft (m)
Iced tea	Iis-tee (m)
Juice	Saft (m)
Mineral water	Mineralwasser (n)
Orange juice	Orangschäsaft (m) / O-Saft (m)
Water with / without gas	Wasser mit / ooni Cholesüüri Wasser mit / ooni Blööterli
Soft drink	Blööterliwasser (n)
Cold chocolate	Chalti Schoggi (f)

 48

Typical Swiss drinks

For children, **haissi Ovi / Ovo** (hot ovaltine).

In summer typical drinks are: **än Gsprüzztä** (white wine with water and lemon), **äs Panaché** (beer with lemonade) or a **Schtangä** (draft beer).

Typical winter drinks include: **Schümli Pflümli** (coffee with spirits and whipped cream), **Kafi Schnaps** (coffee with spirit), **Jägertee** (tea with spirit), **Punsch** (punch), or **Glüäwii** (hot wine).

In autumn you may find **Suser** (half fermented wine).

Food & Drinks

Alcohol	
Beer	Biär (n)
Cider	suurä Moscht (m)
Digestive	Vertailer (m)
	Digestive (m) *(Dischestiv)*
Draft beer	Schtangä (f)
Hot wine	Glüäwii (m)
Spirit	Schnaps (m)
Wine	Wii (m)
Red wine	Rotwii (m)
	Rotä (m)
White wine	Wiisswii (m)
	Wiissä (m)
a glass of Champagne	Güppli (n)

...OH DEAR...
WRONG BOTTLE...

49

Food & Drinks

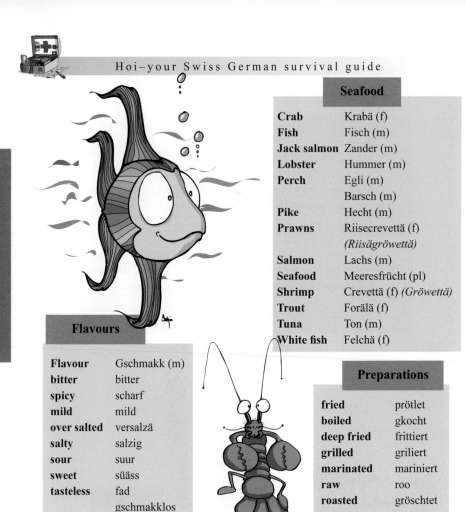

Seafood

Crab	Krabä (f)
Fish	Fisch (m)
Jack salmon	Zander (m)
Lobster	Hummer (m)
Perch	Egli (m)
	Barsch (m)
Pike	Hecht (m)
Prawns	Riisecrevettä (f)
	(Riisägröwettä)
Salmon	Lachs (m)
Seafood	Meeresfrücht (pl)
Shrimp	Crevettä (f) *(Gröwettä)*
Trout	Forälä (f)
Tuna	Ton (m)
White fish	Felchä (f)

Flavours

Flavour	Gschmakk (m)
bitter	bitter
spicy	scharf
mild	mild
over salted	versalzä
salty	salzig
sour	suur
sweet	süäss
tasteless	fad
	gschmakklos

Preparations

fried	prötlet
boiled	gkocht
deep fried	frittiert
grilled	griliert
marinated	mariniert
raw	roo
roasted	gröschtet

Vegetables & Legumes

Beans	Boonä (f)	Lettuce	Chopfsalat (m)
Broccoli	Broggoli (m)	Onion	Zwiblä (f)
Carrots	Rüäbli (n)		Bölä (pl)
Cauliflower	Bluämächöl (m)	Pepper	Pepperoni (f)
Eggplant	Oberschinä (f)	Potatoes	Herdöpfel (m)
Garlic	Chnobli (m)	Salad	Salat (m)
	Chnoblauch (m)	Spinach	Schpinat (m)
Lentils	Linsä (pl)	Tomato	Tomatä (f)
Legumes	Hülsäfrücht (pl)	Vegetables	Gmüäs (n)

50

Typical Swiss Dishes

Chäsfondue *(Chäsfondü)*	Melted Cheese dipped with Bread
Raclette *(Ragglett)*	Melted Cheese, eaten with potatoes
Röschti	Potato tortilla
Zürigschnäzzläts	Sliced meat (e.g. veal) with a cream sauce
Birchermüesli	Muesli with fruit, oats and yoghurt
Vermicelles *(Wermisell)*	Dessert made of chestnuts

Food & Drinks

Other Food

Egg	Ai (n)	**Ice cream**	Glacé (n) *(Glasse)*
Butter	Butter (m)	**Jam**	Gomfi (f)
	Ankä (m)	**Margarine**	Margerinä (f)
Candy	Zältli (n)	**Marmalade**	Orangschägomfi (f)
Condiment	Aromat (n)	**Olive oil**	Olivenöl (n)
	Gwürz (pl)	**Pasta**	Pasta (f)
Corn	Mais (m)		Taigwarä (pl)
Corn on the cob	Mais-cholbä (m)	**Peanut butter**	Erdnussbutter (m)
Dressing	Salatsossä (f)	**Rice**	Riis (m)
Flour	Määl (n)	**Sugar**	Zukker (m)
Honey	Honig (m)	**Vinegar**	Essig (m)

Fruit

Apple	Öpfel (m)
Banana	Bananä (f)
Cherry	Chriäsi (n)
Fruit	Frucht (f)
Lemon	Zitrone (f)
Lime	Limone (f)
Tangerine	Mandarinli (n)
Orange	Orangschä (f)
Pear	Birä (f)
Raspberry	Himbeeri (n)
Strawberry	Erdbeeri (n)
Watermelon	Wassermelonä (f)

Bread

Baguette	Pariserbrot (n)
Bread	Brot (n)
brown bread	dunkels Brot (n)
Cake	Chuächä (m)
Croissant	Gipfeli (n)
Jam doughnut	Berliner (m)
Pastry	Gebäkk (n)
Pie	Wäjä (f)
Roll	Brötli (n) / Pürli (n)
Sandwich	Sandwich (m)
	(Sändwitsch)
Toast	Tooscht (m)
White bread	Wiissbrot (n)
Whole grain bread	Vollkornbrot (n)

Dairy Products

Yoghurt	Joghurt (n)
	(Jogurt)
Cheese	Chäs (m)
Cream	Raam (m)
Curd cheese	Quark (m)
Milk	Milch (f)

Shopping

Groceries	Läbesmittel (pl)
Bakery	Bekk (m)
	Bekkerei (f)
Butcher's shop	Mezzg(erei) (f)
Deli (katessen)	Delikatessladä (m)
fresh	früsch
frozen	tüfgfrorä
Shop	Ladä (m)
shopping	iichauffä
Supermarket	Supermärt (m)
Fruits of the season	aktuelli Frücht
	säsonali Frücht

Diets

Diet	Diät (f)
diabetic	diabetisch
kosher	koscher
halal	halal
vegan	vegan(isch)
vegetarian	vegetarisch

Does the meal contain pork / meat?
Hätt's Schweineflaisch / Flaisch i däm Essä?
Do you have vegetarian dishes?
Händ Sii au Vegi-Menüs?

Food & Drinks

It is also common for a waiter to ask, after a meal, whether the food was good **'Isch äs guät gsi?'** This is not merely a polite question, but an opportunity to bring in some feedback.

In Switzerland, it is common practice to share the bill if you are in a restaurant or bar with someone else. On such occasions, the waiter will usually ask you:

Zaled Sii trännt oder mitenand? (Are you paying separately or together?)
The answer then is:
Trännt bitte (separate) or **Mitenand** (together).

Food & Drinks

WOULD YOU LIKE ME TO SPLIT THE BILL?

Places to Eat

		Canteen	Kantinä (f)
Bar	Bar (f)		Mensa (f)
Restaurant	Reschtorant (n)	**Take away**	Take away (m)
	Baiz (f)		*(Teik Awei)*
Coffee bar/cafe	Kafi (n)	**Dining car**	Schpiiswagä (m)

Health

Key Survival Phrases

I don't feel well.	Ich füül mich nöd wool.
I feel sick.	Mir isch schlächt.
	Ich füül mich chrank.
Where can I find a pharmacy?	Wo hätt's än Apothek?
I need something for…	Ich bruchä n'öppis gägä...
Do I need a prescription?	Bruch ich äs Rezäpt?
I am allergic to…	Ich bin allergisch gägä...
Do you have something for...?	Händ Sii öppis gägä…? (fr)
I need my glasses.	Ich bruchä mini Brülä.
I think I'm going to be sick.	Ich glaub, mir wird schlächt.
I have diarrhoea.	Ich ha Durchfall.
I need a pill.	Ich bruchä ä Tablettä.
I'm bleeding.	Ich blüätä.
That doesn't look very safe.	Das gseet nöd grad sicher us.
I have a headache / toothache.	Ich ha Chopfwee / Zaawee.

Key Survival Phrases

He / she has concussion.	Er / Sii hätt ä Ghirnerschütterig.
fall down / I fell down.	umfallä, umgheiä / Ich bin umgfallä.
	Ich bi gschtürzt.
I stumbled.	Ich bi gschtürchlet / gschtolperet.
I broke my arm / leg / foot.	Ich ha mir dä Arm / s'Bai / dä Fuäss brochä.
My stomach / head / tooth hurts.	Min Magä / Chopf / Zaa tuät wee.
Are you pregnant?	Sind Sii schwanger? (fr)
When was your last period?	Wänn händ Sii sletscht Mal Iri Täg ka? (fr)
Do you take any hormones?	Nämed Sii Hormon? (fr)
Do you take any medicine?	Nämed Sii Medikamänt? (fr)
Do you take drugs?	Nämed Sii Drogä? (fr)
Do you drink alcohol?	Trinked Sii Alkohol? (fr)
Do you smoke?	Rauched Sii? (fr)
Do you have a private insurance?	Sind Sii privat versicheret? (fr)
What health insurance do you have?	Was für ä Chrankäkassä händ Sii? (fr)
Do you have any hereditary illnesses in your family?	Händ Sii Erbchrankhaitä i dä Familiä? (fr)

Health and Safety

Hospital			
Ambulance	Ambulanz (f)	**Patient**	Paziänt (m)
	Chrankäwagä (m)		Paziäntin (f)
Clinic	Klinik (f)	**Prescription**	Rezäpt (n)
Doctor	Arzt (m) / Ärztin (f)	**Ward**	Schtazion(f)
Doctor's surgery	Praxis (f)		Abtailig (f)
Emergency	Notfall (m)	**Intensive care**	Intensivschtazion (f)
Hospital	Schpital (n)	**First Aid**	Erschti Hilf (f)
Emergency room	Notufnaam (f)	**Nurse ***	Chrankäschwöschter (f)

BE AWARE!

* The name for nurse has recently changed from **'Chrankäschwöschter'** (Illness sister) to **'Pflägfachfrau / maa'** (Care specialist). The reason is that the profession has evolved and nurses in Switzerland didn't want to continue being associated with the nun community who were, originally, the ones doing this task.

Health Problems

Abscess	Apszäss (m)	Flu	Grippe (f)
allergic to	alergisch gägä	Hay fever	Hoischnuppä (m)
Allergy	Alergii (f)	Headache	Chopfwee (n)
Appendicitis	Blinddarmenzündig (f)	Infection	Enzündig (f)
Asthma	Aschtma (n)	Injury	Verlezzig (f)
Blood pressure	Bluätdrukk (m)	Insomnia	Schlaflosikait (f)
Blood sugar	Bluätzukker (m)	Pain	Schmärzä (pl)
Broken bone	Chnochäbruch (m)	Parasite	Parasit (m)
burn / burned	verbränä	Poison	Gift (n)
	verbrännt	poisoned	vergiftet
Cold	Vercheltig (f)	Rabies	Tollwuät (f)
Concussion	Ghirnerschütterig (f)	sick	chrank
contagious	aschtekkänd	Stomach ache	Buuchwee (n)
Cramp	Chrampf (m)	Temperature	Temperatur (f)
Diabetes	Diabetis (f)	to cough	huäschtä
Diarrhoea	Durchfall (m)	Virus	Wirus (m)
Fever	Fiäber (n)		

Health Remedies

Aspirin	Aschpirin (n)		
Antidote	Gägägift (n)		
Band-aid	Pfläschterli (n)		
Bandage	Verband (m)		
Condom	Kondom (n)		
Contraceptive	Verhüetigsmittel (n)	Pain Killer	Schmärzmittel (n)
Cream	Crème (f) *(Gräm)*	Pill	Pillä (f)
Drops	Tröpfli (pl)	Sleeping pill	Schlaftablettä (f)
Injection	Schprüzzä (f)	Suppositories	Zäpfli (n)
Massage	Massage (f)*(Masaasch)*	Syrup	Sirup (m)
Medicine	Hailmittel (n)	Tampon	Tampon (m)
Operation	Operazion (f)		

Human Body

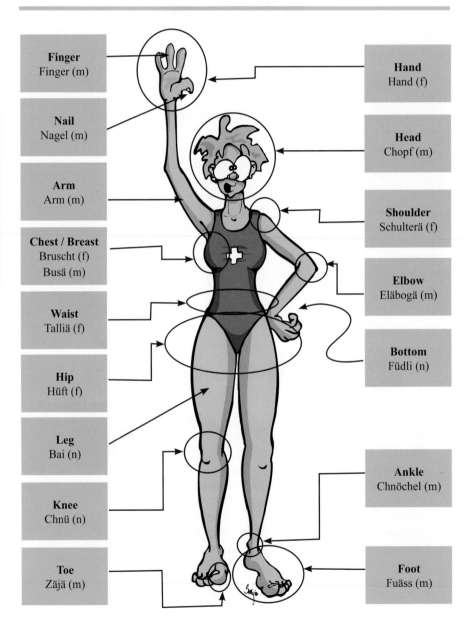

Finger
Finger (m)

Nail
Nagel (m)

Arm
Arm (m)

Chest / Breast
Bruscht (f)
Busä (m)

Waist
Talliä (f)

Hip
Hüft (f)

Leg
Bai (n)

Knee
Chnü (n)

Toe
Zäjä (m)

Hand
Hand (f)

Head
Chopf (m)

Shoulder
Schulterä (f)

Elbow
Eläbogä (m)

Bottom
Füdli (n)

Ankle
Chnöchel (m)

Foot
Fuäss (m)

Health & Safety

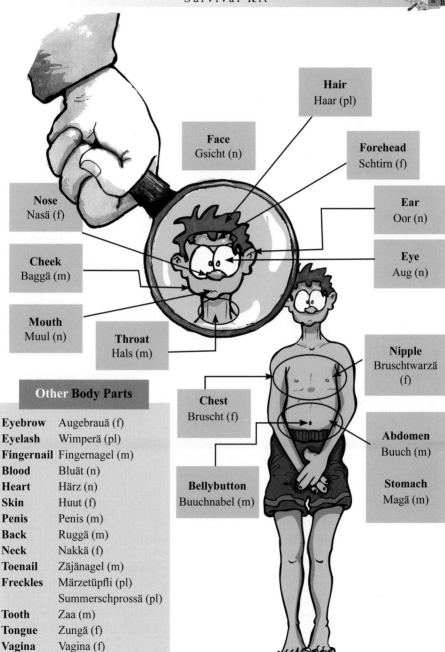

Hair
Haar (pl)

Face
Gsicht (n)

Forehead
Schtirn (f)

Nose
Nasä (f)

Ear
Oor (n)

Cheek
Baggä (m)

Eye
Aug (n)

Mouth
Muul (n)

Throat
Hals (m)

Nipple
Bruschtwarzä (f)

Chest
Bruscht (f)

Abdomen
Buuch (m)

Bellybutton
Buuchnabel (m)

Stomach
Magä (m)

Other Body Parts

Eyebrow	Augebrauä (f)
Eyelash	Wimperä (pl)
Fingernail	Fingernagel (m)
Blood	Bluät (n)
Heart	Härz (n)
Skin	Huut (f)
Penis	Penis (m)
Back	Ruggä (m)
Neck	Nakkä (f)
Toenail	Zäjänagel (m)
Freckles	Märzetüpfli (pl)
	Summerschprossä (pl)
Tooth	Zaa (m)
Tongue	Zungä (f)
Vagina	Vagina (f)

Health & Safety

> **BE AWARE!** In High German smell is **'riechen'** and taste is **'schmecken'**. Swiss German, on the other hand, doesn't distinguish between the two, and uses the verb **'schmökkä'** for both.

Body Activities

Eyes:			babys: görpslä
blink	blinzlä		
cry	brüälä	**Hands:**	
	hüüla	**touch**	berüärä
wink	zwinkerä		aalangä
stare	schtarrä	**press**	drukkä
look / watch	luägä	**hug**	umarmä
see	gsee	**shake**	schüttlä
I am short-sighted.	Ich bi churzsichtig.	**fold**	faltä
I am long-sighted.	Ich bi wiitsichtig.	**pray**	bätä
		hold	hebä
Ears:		**grab**	griiffä
listen	losä		feschthebä
hear	ghörä		
wiggle	gwagglä (mit dä	**Nose:**	
	Oorä gwagglä)	**smell**	schmökkä
		blow one's nose	sich d'Nasä puzzä
Mouth:		**cover**	zuähebä
smile	lächlä		
laugh	lachä	**Skin:**	
whisper	flüschterä	**blush**	root werdä
kiss	küssä	**get wrinkles**	Faltä übercho
lick	lutschä	**dry out**	uuströchnä
suck	sugä	**Goose bumps**	Huänerhuut (f)
speak	redä	**to get goose bumps**	Huänärhuut übercho
yawn	gäänä	**to break out in a rash**	än Uus-schlag
cough	huäschtä		übercho
burp	görpsä		

Emotions

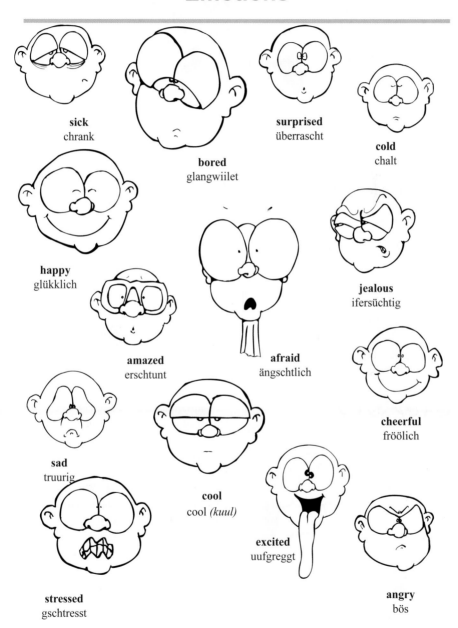

sick
chrank

bored
glangwiilet

surprised
überrascht

cold
chalt

happy
glükklich

jealous
ifersüchtig

amazed
erschtunt

afraid
ängschtlich

cheerful
fröölich

sad
truurig

cool
cool *(kuul)*

excited
uufgreggt

angry
bös

stressed
gschtresst

Health & Safety

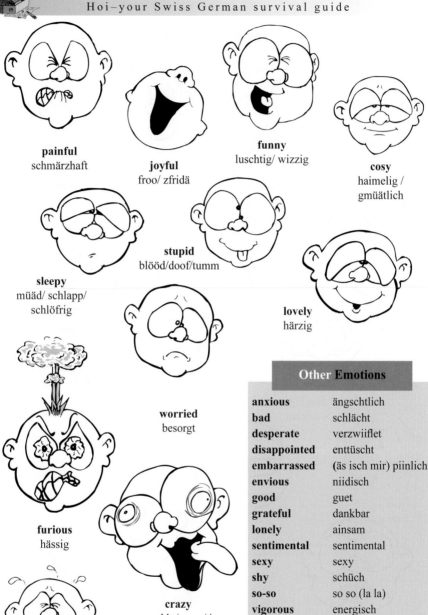

painful
schmärzhaft

joyful
froo/ zfridä

funny
luschtig/ wizzig

cosy
haimelig /
gmüätlich

stupid
blööd/doof/tumm

sleepy
müäd/ schlapp/
schlöfrig

lovely
härzig

worried
besorgt

furious
hässig

crazy
verrukkt/ gaga/ irr

depressed
depressiv

Other Emotions	
anxious	ängschtlich
bad	schlächt
desperate	verzwiiflet
disappointed	enttüscht
embarrassed	(äs isch mir) piinlich
envious	niidisch
good	guet
grateful	dankbar
lonely	ainsam
sentimental	sentimental
sexy	sexy
shy	schüch
so-so	so so (la la)
vigorous	energisch
horny	schpizz
	giggerig

Swiss Expressions

Deciphering Swiss expressions may be a challenge; therefore, the following illustrations can be used as a guideline:

$=$ HAPPY
glükklich

$=$ SAD
truurig

$=$ ANGRY
bös

$=$ COOL
cool
(kuul)

$=$ CRAZY
verrukkt/ gaga/
irr

Health and Safety

Emergency

Emergencies

An avalanche!	Ä Lawinä!
Be careful!	Achtung!
Call an ambulance!	Ruäfed Sii än Chrankäwagä! (fr)
	Rüäf än Chrankäwagä! (inf)
Call the police!	Lütet Sii dä Polizai a! (fr)
	Lüt dä Polizai a! (inf)
Can someone call a doctor?	Chann öpper amenä Arzt aalütä?
Someone is following me!	Öpper verfolgt mich!
Fire!	Füür!
Help!	Hilfe (f)!
Hurry!	Schnäll!
I am a diabetic.	Ich bi Diabetiker / in.
She is pregnant.	Sii isch schwanger.
I am pregnant.	Ich bi schwanger.
Is there a doctor?	Isch än Arzt da?
It's an emergency!	Äs isch än Notfall!
Jump!	Gump!
Get out of the way!	Gönd Sii wäg! (fr)
	Gönd Sii uf Ziitä! (fr)
	Gang wäg! (inf)
	Gang uf Ziitä! (inf)
Run!	Ränned Sii! (fr)
	Ränn! (inf)
Thief!	Diäb!
Watch out!	Passed Sii uuf! (fr)
	Pass uuf! (inf)
We need a doctor!	Mir bruched än Arzt!
Where is the nearest pharmacy?	Wo isch di nächscht Apothek?

BE AWARE!

Fürweer (f)   Fire Dept.
Polizai (f)   Police
Notfall (m)   Emergency

Health & Safety

Police

Police

Someone stole my wallet.	Mis Portmonee isch gschtolä wordä.
I want to report a stolen…	Ich möcht mis gschtolne… meldä.
You should go to the police.	Sii söttet zu dä Polizai gaa. (fr)
	Du söttsch zu dä Polizai gaa. (inf)
Can you please call the police?	Chönd Sii bitte dä Polizai aalütä? (fr)
I've been robbed!	Ich bi beschtolä wordä!
I saw what happened.	I ha gsee, was passiert isch.
What's the fine for?	Für was isch diä Puäss?
How much is the fine?	Wiä vill choschtet diä Puäss?
Where is the police station?	Wo isch dä nächscht Polizaiposchtä?

Health and Safety

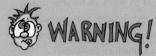 WARNING!

Some of the most common stolen items are:

Wallet	Portmonee (n)
Bicycle	Velo (n) *(Welo)*
Briefcase	Mappä (f)
Bag	Täschä (f)
Purse	Handtäschli (n)
Laptop	Laptop (m) *(Läptop)*
Mobile / Cellular	Händi (n)
	Natel (n)

(In the Money section of the book you can find more useful words.)

POLIZEI

Health & Safety

Immigration & **Customs**

Permit	Bewilligung (f)
	Genemigung (f)
Visa	Wisum (n)
Foreigner	Ussländer/in (m/f)
Customs	Zoll (m)
Frontier / Border	Gränzä (f)
to declare (at customs)	verzollä
to immigrate	iiraisä
to emigrate	uusraisä
a valid visa	äs gültigs Wisum
renew a visa	äs Wisum verlängerä

Residence permit	Ufenthaltsgenemigung (f)
to apply for a visa	äs Wisum beaträgä
What kind of a visa do you have?	Was für äs Wisum händ Sii? (fr)
I want to work in Switzerland.	Ich möcht i dä Schwiiz schaffä.
How can I apply for a visa?	Wiä chann ich äs Wisum beaträgä?
I have something to declare.	Ich ha öppis z'verzollä.
I have nothing to declare.	Ich ha nüt z'verzollä.
Do you have anything to declare?	Händ Sii öppis z'verzollä? (fr)
I want to stay in Switzerland for 3 months.	Ich möcht drü Mönät i dä Schwiiz bliibä.

I am married to a Swiss. Ich bi mit ämä Schwiizer ghüratä (with a Swiss man).
Ich bi mit ärä Schwiizerin ghüratä (with a Swiss woman).

The most common permits for foreigners in Switzerland are:

1. **C-Permit (C-Bewilligung), Niderlassigsbewilligung:** unlimited residency in Switzerland.
2. **B-Permit (B-Bewilligung), Jaaresbewilligung:** usually has to be renewed each year.
3. **L-Permit (L-Bewilligung) :** Short-term Work or Residence Permit.
4. **G-Permit Gränzgänger-Bewilligung:** border crosser permit.
5. **Turischtäwisum** (Tourist Visa): usually valid for three months.

Shopping in General

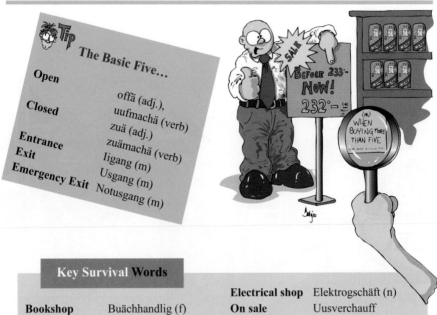

The Basic Five...

Open	offä (adj.), uufmachä (verb)
Closed	zuä (adj.) zuämachä (verb)
Entrance	Iigang (m)
Exit	Usgang (m)
Emergency Exit	Notusgang (m)

Key Survival Words

		Electrical shop	Elektrogschäft (n)
Bookshop	Buächhandlig (f)	On sale	Uusverchauff
	Büächerladä (m)	Price	Priis (m)
Brand	Markä (f)	Security	Sicherhait (f)
Cashier	Kassierer (m)	Shopping bag	Iichaufs-Täschä (f)
	Kassiererin (f)	Store	Ladä (m)
complain	sich beklagä /chlönä	Shopping centre	Ichaufszentrum (n)
	mozzä	to buy	poschtä, chauffä
Department	Abtailig (f)	to order	pschtelä
Discount	reduziert	to sell	verchauffä

BE AWARE! The biggest retailers in Switzerland own not only supermarkets, but also a vast variety of other types of shops. As they all have the same 'customer incentive' strategies, it is most likely that some shops will ask you before you pay if you have their shopping card, which allows customers to collect bonus points for every purchase.

Key Survival Shopping Phrases

to go shopping	lädälä
Do you have...?	Händ Sii…? (fr)
I'm looking for…	Ich suächä…
How much does it cost?	Wiä vill choschtet das?
How much does this cost?	Wiä vill choschtet das? Wiä tüür isch das?
At what time do you open?	Wänn mached Sii uuf?
At what time do you close?	Wänn mached Sii zuä?
	Ab wänn händ Sii zuä?
Do you have something cheaper?	Git's au öppis Günschtigers?
That's expensive!	Das isch tüür!
Can you give me…?	Chönd Sii mir … gä? (fr)
Do you accept credit cards?	Nämed Sii Kreditchartä? (fr)
I need a shopping bag.	Ich bruchä än Plastiksakk / ä Tragtäschä.
I would like to try it on.	Chann ich das mal probierä?
How long is the warranty / guarantee?	Wiä lang gits Garantii?
I want my money back!	Ich will mis Gäld zrugg!
I will take this.	Ich nimm das.
I'm just browsing.	Ich luägä nu echli.
Where is the exit?	Wo isch dä Notusgang?
Do you have a larger / smaller size?	Händ Sii das au grösser? chlinner?(fr)
Can you please give me a receipt?	Chönd Sii mir ä Quittig gee? (fr)

Shopping

… A SWISS GERMAN DICTIONARY?…
YES, UPSTAIRS, IN THE CROSSWORDS AND
PUZZLE SECTION…

BOOKS

Clothes

Shopping

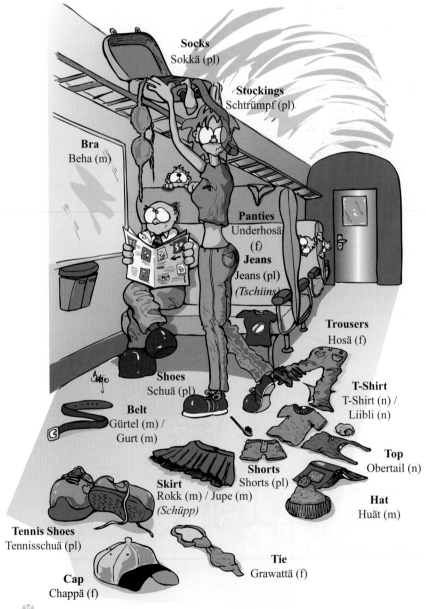

Clothes & Accessories

Blouse	Blusä (f)	Gloves	Häntschä (pl)
Button	Chnopf (m)	Jacket	Jagge (f)
Clothing	Chlaider (pl)	Scarf	Schal (m) / Tuäch (n)
Coat	Mantel (m)	Shirt	Hämp (n)
Collar	Chragä (m)	short sleeves	churzärmlig
Suit	Koschtüm (n)	long sleeves	langärmlig
Dress (noun)	Chlaid (n)	Underwear	Underwösch (f)
dress (verb)	aaziiä	Wallet	Portmonee (n)
dressed	aazogä		
Evening dress	Aabigchlaid (n)		

Shopping

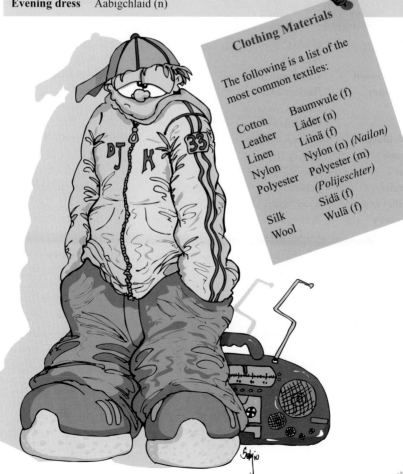

Clothing Materials

The following is a list of the most common textiles:

Cotton	Baumwule (f)
Leather	Läder (n)
Linen	Linä (f)
Nylon	Nylon (n) (Nailon)
Polyester	Polyester (m) (Polijeschter)
Silk	Sidä (f)
Wool	Wulä (f)

Money & Banking

Shopping

Money

Money	Gäld (n)	invest money	Gäld inweschtierä
Bank	Bank (f)	Investment	Inweschtizion (f)
Bank account	Bankkonto (n)		Inweschtierig (f)
Banknotes	Banknotä (f)	Loan	Darleä (n)
Cash	Cash (n) *(Käsch)*	Loss	Verluscht (m)
	Bargäld (n)	Payment	Zalig (f)
Cash machine	Gäldautomat (m)	Profit	Profit (m)
Cheque	Schegg (m)	Rappen *	Rappä (m)
Coin	Münzä (f)	Savings account	Schparkonto (n)
Counter	Schalter (m)	Signature	Unterschrift (f)
Credit card	Kreditchartä (f)	Small change	Münz (n)
Currency	Wäärig (f)	Swiss franc	Schwiizer Frankä (m)
Debit card	EC-Chartä (f) *(Eze-*	to pay	zalä
	Chartä)	to save	schparä
	Poschtchartä (f)	to spend	uusgä
Deposit	Depot (n) *(Depo)*	to transfer	überwiisä
	Hinderlegig (f)	Travellers' cheques	Traveller cheques (pl)
earn money	Gäld verdiänä		*(Träwälär Schegg)*
Exchange rate	Wächselratä (f)	to withdraw	abhebä
Income	Iikomä (n)		
Interest	Zins (m)	* 100 Rappen = 1 Swiss Franc	

Money, Banks and Exchange Office

What's the exchange rate today for British pounds / dollars?
Wiä isch dä Wächselkurs für Britischi Pfund / Dollar hüt?

Can you please change this banknote for small change?
Chönd Sii mir das Nötli wechslä? (fr)

Do you have change for this?
Chönd Sii mir das i Münz wächslä? (fr)

I don't have any money.
Ich ha kai Gäld.

Your cash machine kept my card!
Dä Gäldautomat hätt mini Chartä iäzogä!

How many francs do I get for X dollars ?
Wiä vill frankä chumm ich für X Dollar über?

I would like to open a bank account / savings account.
Ich möcht äs Bankkonto/ Schparkonto erröffnä.

to put money aside
Gäld schparä / Gäld uf Ziitä legä / Gäld uf di höch Kantä legä

Shopping

Transportation

A ticket to..., please.	Äs Bilet uf ..., bitte.
How much does a ticket to...cost?	Wiä vill choschtet s'Bilet uf...?
Window / aisle	Am Fänschter / bim Gang
No Smoking	Nichtraucher
single / one way ticket	nur hii / aifach
Return ticket	hii und zrugg / hii und retour *(rötur)*
Do I have to change trains?	Muäs ich umschtigä?
Where do I have to change...?	Wo muäs ich umschtiigä?
The train / bus is delayed.	Dä Zug / Bus hätt Verschpötig.
on foot	z`Fuäss
by car / by bike	mit äm Auto / Velo
by plane / by train	mit äm Flugzüg / mit äm Zug
The flight is cancelled.	Dä Flug isch anuliert.
Where can I get a taxi?	Wo hätt's äs Taxi?

Key Survival Phrases

Continued on the next page....

Traveling

74

Key Survival Phrases

I have lost my ticket.	Ich ha mis Bilet verlorä.
I bought the wrong ticket.	Ich ha s`falsch Bilet kauft.
Does this train / bus stop at…?	Haltet dä Zug / Bus bi.. / in..?
When does the next train for...leave?	Wänn faart dä nächschti Zug uf...?
Is this the train / bus to….?	Isch das dä Zug / Bus uf...?
At what time does the train from…arrive?	Wänn chunnt dä Zug vo...aa?
On what platform does the next train for... leave?	Uf welläm Glais faart dä Zug uf…?

WARNING!

What Ticket Controllers Will Usually Ask...

Ali Bilet bitte!
All tickets please (request to show tickets)
Wohär chömed Sii? / Wo sind Sii iigstigä?
Where are you coming from?
Wo anä faared Sii?
Where are you going?
Händ Sii äs gültigs Bilet?
Do you have a valid ticket?

BE AWARE! All public announcements over the loudspeakers are made in High-German. Only on very rare occasions is Swiss German used.

Tip There are different tickets with special price offers to travel around Switzerland. The main offers are:

GA (n) (Generalabonnement): an unlimited ticket valid for most of public transport in Switzerland.
Halbtax (n): a card that allows you to buy tickets for most public transport at half price.
Tages-chartä (f): a 'one-day ticket' valid for most of public transport in Switzerland.
Familiä-chartä (f): a ticket for families, which offers reduced prices for children.

Website: **www.sbb.ch/en**

Nächster Halt: "MILANO"

DEUTSCH

Traveling

Traveling

Travel Words

		to reserve	reservierä
Aeroplane	Flugzüg (n)	Tourist	Turischt (m)
Arrival	Akunft (f)		Turischtin (f)
Bus	Bus (m)	Train	Zug (m)
Bus stop	Bushalteschtell (f)	Train ticket	Zugbilet (n)
Bus ticket	Busbilet (n)	Train station	Baanhof (m)
Car	Auto (n)	Bus station	Busbaanhof (m)
City map	Schtadtplan (m)	Track	Glais (n)
Delay	Verschpötig (f)	Platform	Perron (n)
Departure	Abrais (f)	Petrol station	Tankschtell (f)
Driver's licence	Faaruuswis (m)	Service area	Raschtplazz (m)
	Bilet (n)		Raschtschtettä (f)
Plane ticket	Flugzüg-Tikket (n)	Speed camera	Radar (m)
Highway/Motorway	Autobaan (f)	drive too fast	rasä
Luggage	Gepäkk (n)	leave	abfaarä
Passenger	Passagier (m)	land	landä
	(Passaschier)	to get on a bus	In Bus iischtigä
Passport	Pass (m)	to get off a bus	Us äm Bus uusschtigä
Petrol	Bänzin (n)	Speed limit	Gschwindigkaits-
Rucksack	Rukksakk (m)		begränzig (f)
Space	Ruum (m)		

Directions

to the left	nach linggs
to the right	nach rächts
around (the corner)	um (dä Eggä)
across (the bridge, the crossover)	über (d'Brugg, d'Überfüerig)
(X) streets from here	(X) Schtrassä wiitär
I'm looking for…	Ich suächä...
I think I am lost.	Ich glaub, ich ha mich verloffä.
Where? / in which direction?	wo? / i wellerä Richtig?
Do you know where... is?	Wüssed Sii, wo ... isch? (fr)
	Waisch du, wo ... isch? (inf)
Could you tell me the way to ….?	Chönted Sii mir sägä, wo ....isch? (fr)
How far is it to walk / to drive?	Wiä wiit isch äs zum Lauffä / zum Faarä?
Go straight on as far as the church.	Gönd Sii graduus bis zu dä Chilä. (fr)
Go along by the river.	Lauffed Sii am Fluss entlang. (fr)
along the street	dä Schtrass entlang

Continued on the next page….

Traveling

Key Survival Phrases

Go up! / Go down!	Gönd Sii ufä! (fr)
	Gönd Sii abä! (fr)
up the stairs	d'Schtägä ufä
down the escalator	d'Rollträppä abä
go across the street	Gönd Sii über d'Schtrass. (fr)
Is it far / close?	Isch äs wiit / nöch?
behind the house	hinder s'Huus
in front of the house	vor s'Huus
through the market	dur dä Märt
to the station / to the church	bis zum Baanhof / zu dä Chilä
passing the school	a dä Schuäl verbii
leaving the village	us äm Dorf usä
entering the village	is Dorf inä
not far at all	nur än Chazzäschprung *
	nöd wiit

* only a stone's throw

Some Reference Points

Bridge	Brugg (f)
Cathedral	Katedraale (f)
Church	Chilä (f)
Corner	Eggä (m)
Crossing	Chrüüzig (f)
Mosque	Moschee (f)
School	Schuäl (f)
Street	Schtrass (f)
Synagogue	Synagogä (f)
Traffic light	Amplä (f)

Key Words

up	ufä
down	abä
left	linggs
right	rächts
here	da
there	deet
straight on	graduus
Map	Chartä (f)
	Schtadtplan (f)

Prepositions

When it comes to directions, prepositions are the most useful words to provide accurate information. This list shows the most common prepositions in Swiss German.

Key Prepositions

from	us	until / by	bis
with / by (transport)	mit	at / on (vertical surfaces)	a(m)
from / of	vo	on (horizontal surfaces)	uf
at / by	bi	behind	hinder
after / according to	nach	in / into	in
to	zu	beside / next to	näbäd
across from / opposite	gägänüber	over / above / across	über
through	dur(ch)	under / beneath	under
against / into	gägä	in front of	vor
around	um	between	zwüschä
for	für	along	entlang
without	ooni		

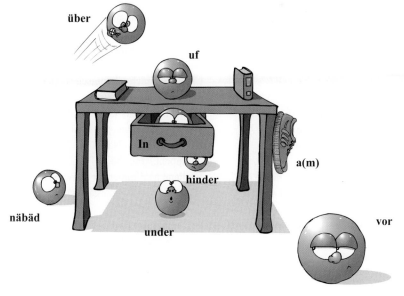

Traveling

79

Hotel

Traveling

Key Survival Phrases

Do you have a room?	Händ Sii no Zimmer frei? (fr)
Single / Double room please.	Äs Ainzelzimmer / äs Doppelzimmer, bitte.
Is breakfast included?	Isch dä Zmorgä im Priis inbegriffä?
with a view of the lake.	mit Seesicht
Can I have a morning call?	Chönd Sii mich telefonisch wekkä?
I want to check out.	Ich möcht uus-tschäggä.
Can I have the key to the room?	Dä Schlüssel fürs Zimmer...,bitte.
How much is it a night?	Wiä vill choschtets pro Nacht?
I will stay for.....nights.	Ich bliibe für .... Nächt.
I'd like to book...	Ich möcht... buächä.
I reserved a room in the name of....	Ich hann äs Zimmer für ... reserviert.
At what time is breakfast served?	Wänn chammär Zmorgä ässä?
a quiet room	äs ruigs Zimmer
a room with bath / with bath nearby	äs Zimmer mit Bad
	mit Etageduschi *(Etascheduschi)*
Youth hostel	Jugendhärbärg (f)

Survival Kit

Hotel Words

B&B	B&B (n)	**Wake up call**	Wekkaaruäf (m)
Bed	Bett (n)	**Pillow**	Chüssi (n)
Bed cover	Bettaazug (m)	**Reception**	Rezepzion (f)
Check in	iitschäggä	**Room**	Zimmer (n)
Check out	uus-tschäggä	**Room service**	Zimmerservice (m)
Concierge	Consierge (m)		*(Zimmer-Serwis)*
	(Gonsiersch)	**Slippers**	Finkä (pl)
Double bed	Doppelbett (n)	**Swimming pool**	Schwümmbad (n)
Gym	Fitnessruum (m)	**Towel**	Tüächli (n)
Key	Schlüssel (m)	**Full board**	Vollpension (f)
Lift	Lift (m)	**Half board**	Halbpension (f)
Lobby	Lobbi (f)		

Traveling

81

Outdoors

Traveling

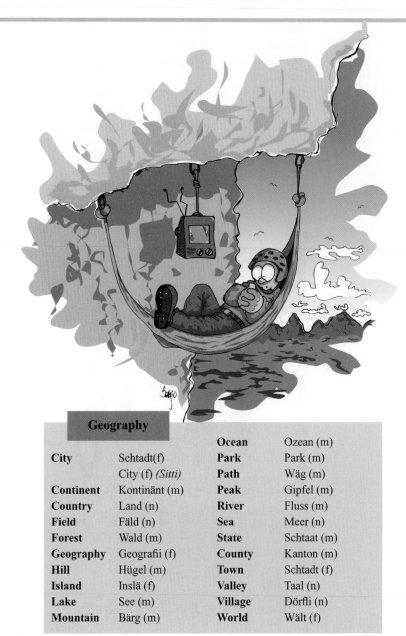

Geography

		Ocean	Ozean (m)
City	Schtadt(f)	**Park**	Park (m)
	City (f) *(Sitti)*	**Path**	Wäg (m)
Continent	Kontinänt (m)	**Peak**	Gipfel (m)
Country	Land (n)	**River**	Fluss (m)
Field	Fäld (n)	**Sea**	Meer (n)
Forest	Wald (m)	**State**	Schtaat (m)
Geography	Geografii (f)	**County**	Kanton (m)
Hill	Hügel (m)	**Town**	Schtadt (f)
Island	Inslä (f)	**Valley**	Taal (n)
Lake	See (m)	**Village**	Dörfli (n)
Mountain	Bärg (m)	**World**	Wält (f)

Outdoor Snow Terms

Skiing	schiifaarä	pretty girl skiing	Schneehäsli (n)
I like skiing.	Ich faarä gärn Schii.	Snowboard	snöbä bordä Snowboard faarä *(Snoubord)*
Ski lift	Schiilift (m)		
Chair lift	Sässelilift (m)		
easy hill to ski	Idiotähügel (m)	Equipment	Uusrüschtig (f)
Ski	Schii (m)	Snow shoeing	Schneeschuä lauffä
Ski boot	Schiischuä (m)	Cross country skiing	langloifflä
Ski school	Schiischuäl (f)	Ski tour	Schiiturä machä
Ski instructor	Schiileerer (m) Schiileererin (f)	Ski poles	Schtökk (pl)

Traveling

Other Snow Terms & Phrases

Partying and drinking after skiing	Après-ski (n) *(Aprä-Schii)*
Are you a good snowboarder?	Chasch du guät snowboard faarä? (inf)
I am a snowboarder.	Ich bin än Snöbär.
off the marked slope	ab dä Pischtä

Outdoor Mountain Terms

hike	wanderä
Hiking shoes	Wanderschuä (pl)
Grill area	Füürschtell (f)
Elevation gain	Höämeter (m)
Provisions	Proviant (m)
Direction sign	Wägwiiser (m)
Swiss army knife	Sakkmässer (n)
Hiking path	Wanderwäg (m)
Picnic	Picnic (n) *(Piknik)*
Bicycle	Velo (n) *(Welo)*
camping	Camping (n) *(Kämping)*
walking	lauffä
driving	Auto faarä
paragliding	Glaitschirm flügä

Tip

1. If you are a keen hiker or an outdoor person, be sure to become a member of **Rega (Swiss air rescue).** *

2. Hiking trails **(Wanderwäg)** in Switzerland are always marked with a yellow rhombus.

* website: **www.rega.ch/en**

Other Mountain Terms & Phrases

Is it steep?	Isch äs schtail?
How long do we have to climb?	Wiä lang müämmär ufelauffä?
How far away is the restaurant?	Wiä wiit isch äs no bis zu dä Baiz?

Entertainment

Key Survival Phrases

What are your hobbies?	Was sind Iri Hobis? (fr)
	Was sind dini Hobis? (inf)
What do you do in your spare time?	Was mached Sii i Irerä Freiziit? (fr)
	Was machsch i dinerä Freiziit? (inf)
What do you like to do the most?	Was mached Sii am liäbschtä? (fr)
	Was machsch am liäbschtä? (inf)
I like cooking / eating / travelling.	Ich chochä / ässä / raisä gärn.
What's your favourite food?	Was isch dis Liäblingsässä? (inf)
I collect stamps.	Ich sammlä Briäfmarkä.
I like listening to music / watching TV.	Ich losä gärn Musig / Ich luäg gärn Fernse.
I read novels/ cartoons / the newspaper.	Ich läsä Romän / Comics / d'Ziitig.
I listen to classical music.	Ich losä klassischi Musig.
I jog regularly.	Ich tschoggä regelmässig.
I go twice a week to the gym.	Ich gang (zwaimal pro Wuchä) is Fitness.
I like playing golf / the piano / the violin.	Ich schpilä gärn Golf / Klavir / Giigä.

Traveling

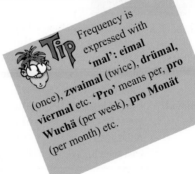

Frequency is expressed with 'mal': **eimal** (once), **zwaimal** (twice), **drümal**, **viermal** etc. **'Pro'** means per, **pro Wuchä** (per week), **pro Monät** (per month) etc.

For preferences, most Swiss use the adverb **'gärn'**, which is always placed after the verb: **Ich ässä gärn Bananä** (I like eating bananas).

Traveling

Key Survival Words

Book	Buäch (n)	Library	Bibliothek (f)
Concert	Konzärt (n)	Humour	Humoor (m)
to collect (cars)	(Auto) sammlä	Joke	Wizz (m)
dancing	tanzä	Magic	Zauberai (f)
dating	deitä		zaubärä (Verb)
Entertainment	Unterhaltig (f)	Museum	Museum (n)
Event	Event (m) *(iwent)*	Music	Musig (f)
	Aalass (m)	Opera	Operä (f)
Exhibition	Uus-schtellig (f)	Party	Party (f) *(Parti)*
to fish	fischä		Fäscht (n)
	anglä	to play	schpilä /geimä
Fitness	Fitness	to play football	tschutä
Beach	Schtrand (m)	to read	läsä
Cinema	Kino (n)	to swim	schwümä
Discotheque	Disco (f)	Theatre	Theater (n)
to gamble	schpilä / gämblä	Wind surfing	Wind sörfä
Game	Schpiil (n)	Zoo	Zoo (m)

Liäblings means
favourite and
can be combined
with lots of
other words: **Liäblings-ässä**
(favourite food), **Liäblings-film**
(favourite movie), **Liäblings-
reschtorant** (favourite
restaurant).

 Swiss Traditions

Carnival	Fasnacht (f)
blowing the alpenhorn	Alp-horn blasä
swinging flags	Faanäschwingä
Crossbow (shooting)	Armbruscht (schüssä)
milking	mälchä
Wood carving	schnizzä
yodelling	jodlä
Swiss wrestling	schwingä
throwing stones	Schtai stossä
swinging coins	Taler schwingä
Swiss accordion	Handörgeli (n)
making cheese	chäsä
Swiss traditional music	Ländler (m)

Traveling

Family

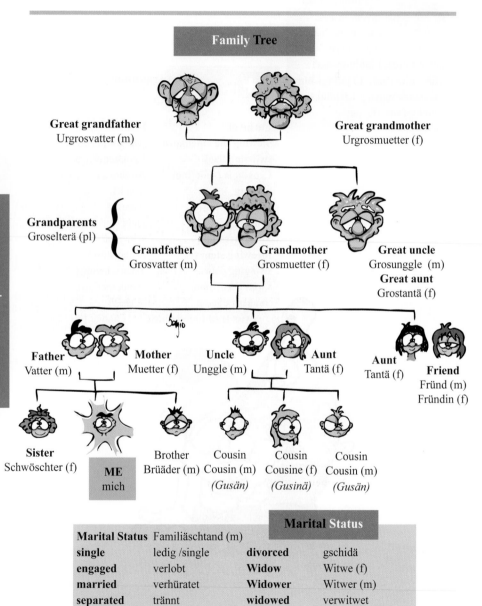

Family Tree

Great grandfather
Urgrosvatter (m)

Great grandmother
Urgrosmuetter (f)

Grandparents
Groselterä (pl)

Grandfather
Grosvatter (m)

Grandmother
Grosmuetter (f)

Great uncle
Grosunggle (m)
Great aunt
Grostantä (f)

Father
Vatter (m)

Mother
Muetter (f)

Uncle
Unggle (m)

Aunt
Tantä (f)

Aunt
Tantä (f)

Friend
Fründ (m)
Fründin (f)

Sister
Schwöschter (f)

ME
mich

Brother
Brüäder (m)

Cousin
Cousin (m)
(Gusän)

Cousin
Cousine (f)
(Gusinä)

Cousin
Cousin (m)
(Gusän)

Marital Status

Marital Status	Familiäschtand (m)		
single	ledig /single	divorced	gschidä
engaged	verlobt	Widow	Witwe (f)
married	verhüratet	Widower	Witwer (m)
separated	trännt	widowed	verwitwet

People

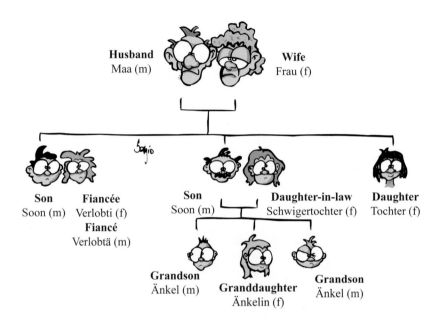

Husband Maa (m)		**Wife** Frau (f)
Son Soon (m)	**Fiancée** Verlobti (f) **Fiancé** Verlobtä (m)	**Son** Soon (m) · **Daughter-in-law** Schwigertochter (f) · **Daughter** Tochter (f)
	Grandson Änkel (m) · **Granddaughter** Änkelin (f) · **Grandson** Änkel (m)	

Other Family Relations

Brother-in-law	Schwager (m)
Father-in-law	Schwigervatter (m)
Grandchild	Gros-chind (n)
Mother-in-law	Schwigermuetter (f)
Nephew	Näffä (m)
Niece	Nichtä (f)
Relatives	Verwandti (pl)
Siblings	Gschwüschterti (pl)
Sister-in-law	Schwögerin (f)
Son-in-law	Schwigersoon (m)
Twins	Zwilling (pl)

People

People

Useful Family Terms

Family get together	Familiäzämäkunft (f)
	Familiäschluuch (m)
We are related.	Mir sind verwandt.
My family is important to me.	Mini Familiä isch mir wichtig.
I am a family person.	Ich bin än Familiämänsch.
My brother's name is…	Min Brüäder haisst…
Parent's home	Elterähuus (n)
My family lives in...	Mini Familiä läbt in…
Give my regards to your family.	Grüäss dini Familiä vo mir. (inf)
How is your family?	Wiä gat's dinerä Familiä? (inf)
We are going to have a baby!	Mir chömed äs Chind über!

BE AWARE!

Possessives are a bit more complicated than in English. Not only is the possessor's gender marked, but also the possessed gender. For example:

He is **my** brother	Er isch **min** Brüäder
She is **my** sister	Sii isch **mini** Schwöschter
She is **his** sister	Sii isch **sini** Schwöschter
She is **her** sister	Sii isch **iri** Schwöschter
He is **his** brother	Er isch **sin** Brüäder
He is **her** brother	Er isch **irä** Brüäder

For a better understanding of the possessive pronouns, check the tables in the Appendix.

Age

Baby boy
Büäbli (n)

Baby girl
Maitli (n)

Boy
Buäb (m)

Teenager
Teeni (m) *(Tiini)*

Girl
Mait(ä)li (n)

Adult
Erwachsenä (m)

Young woman
jungi Frau (f)
Frölain (n)

Young man
Purscht (m)
jungä Maa (m)

Adult
Erwachseni (f)

Old woman
alti Frau (f)

Old man
altä Maa (m)

People

93

Home

House
Huus (n)

Chimney
Chämi (n)

Satellite Dish
Satellitäschüsslä (f)

Roof
Tach (n)

Tree
Baum (m)

Curtains
Vorhäng
(pl)

Window
Fänschter
(n)

Gutter
Tachrinnä (f)

Wall
Wand (f)

Sunshade
Sunätach (n)

Balcony
Balkon
(m)

Door
Tüür (f)

Stairs
Schtägä (f)

Garden
Gartä (m)

Mailbox
Briäfchaschtä
(m)

Footpath
Wäg (m)

Lawn
Rasä (m)

Lawnmower
Rasämäier (m)

Housing

94

Parts of the **House**

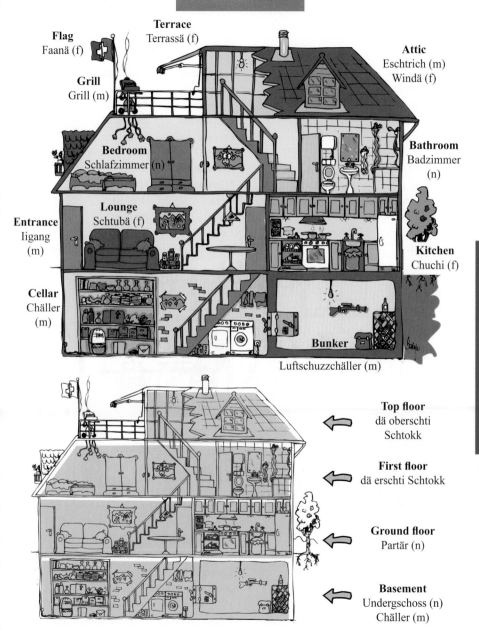

Flag
Faanä (f)

Terrace
Terrassä (f)

Attic
Eschtrich (m)
Windä (f)

Grill
Grill (m)

Bedroom
Schlafzimmer (n)

Bathroom
Badzimmer
(n)

Entrance
Iigang
(m)

Lounge
Schtubä (f)

Kitchen
Chuchi (f)

Cellar
Chäller
(m)

Bunker
Luftschuzzchäller (m)

Top floor
dä oberschti
Schtokk

First floor
dä erschti Schtokk

Ground floor
Partär (n)

Basement
Undergschoss (n)
Chäller (m)

Housing

95

Kitchen Utensils

Bowl	Schüsslä (f)	**Pan**	Pfanä (f)
Box	Schachtlä (f)	**Dinner service**	Tischset (n)
	Chischtä (f)	**Spoon**	Löffel (m)
Cup	Tassä (f)	**Table mats**	Tischmattä (f)
Cutlery	Pschtekk (n)	**Table cloth**	Tischtuäch (n)
Dishes	Gschirr (n)	**Teaspoon**	Teelöffeli (n)
Faucet / tap	Haanä (m)	**Dishwasher**	Abwäschmaschine (f)
Fork	Gablä (f)	**Freezer**	Tüfchüäler (m)
Frying pan	Bratpfanä (f)	**Fridge**	Chüälschrank (m)
Glass	Glas (n)	**Rubbish bin**	Apfall(chübel) (m)
Jam jar	Gomfiglas (n)	**Microwave**	Mikrowälä (f)
Kitchen shelves	Chuchiablagä (pl)	**Oven**	Ofä (m)
Knife	Mässer (n)	**Stove**	Härd (m)
Napkin	Serviettä (f)	**Table**	Tisch (m)
Plate	Täller (m)	**Chair**	Schtuäl (m)

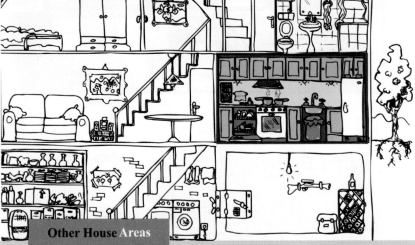

Other House Areas

Entry way	Iigangshallä (f)	**old building**	Altbau (m)
Hallway	Gang (m)	**new building**	Noibau (m)
Lobby	Vorhallä (f)	**Building**	Geboide (n)
	Vorruum (m)	**Garage**	Garasch (f) *(Garasch)*
Dining room	Ässzimmer (n)	**Basement garage**	Tüüfgarage (f)
Floor	Bodä (m)		*(Tüüfgarasch)*
Utility room	Apschtellruum (m)	**Children's room**	Chinderzimmer (n)

Housing

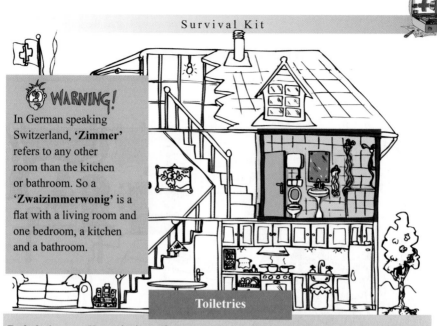

> **WARNING!**
>
> In German speaking Switzerland, **'Zimmer'** refers to any other room than the kitchen or bathroom. So a **'Zwaizimmerwonig'** is a flat with a living room and one bedroom, a kitchen and a bathroom.

Toiletries

Body lotion	Körperlozioon (f)	**Toilet paper**	WC-Papier (n)
Brush	Bürschtä (f)		*(Weze-Papier)*
Comb	Schträäl (m)	**Toiletries**	Badzimmersachä (pl)
Deodorant	Deo (m)	**Toothbrush**	Zaabürschteli (n)
Hand cream	Handcreme (f) *(Handgräm)*	**Toothpaste**	Zaapaschtä (f)
Make-up	Schminkzüg (n)	**Towel**	Tüächli (n)
Razor blades	Rasiärklingä (f)	**Shower**	Duschi (f)
Scales	Waag (f)	**Mirror**	Schpiägel (m)
Shampoo	Schampoo (n)	**Bath tub**	Badwannä (f)
Shower cream	Duschmittel (n)	**Washbasin**	Brüneli (n)
Soap	Soiffä (f)	**Shower curtain**	Duschvorhang (m)
Toiletry bag	Necessaire (n)*(Nessessär)*		

Other Things in the House

Wardrobe	Gardärobä (f)	**Key**	Schlüssel (m)
Book shelves	Büächergschtell (n)	**Pillow**	Chüssi (n)
Carpet	Teppich (m)	**Plug**	Schtekker (m)
Closet	Chaschtä (m)	**Remote control**	Fernbediänig (f)
Desk	Pult (n)	**Sheet**	Bettuäch (n)
Drawer	Schubladä (f)	**Doorbell**	Huusgloggä (f)
Duvet	Bettdekki (f)	**Iron**	Bügälisä (n)
Hanger	Chlaiderbügel (m)		

Housing

Neighbours & Agencies

Looking for a Flat

Furnished room / furnished flat	möblierts Zimmer / möblierti Wonig (f)
Quiet area	ruigi Lag (f)
List of deficiencies	Mängellischtä (f)
I am looking for a cheap flat.	Ich suächä ä billigi Wonig.
Is the flat quiet / big / sunny?	Isch d'Wonig ruig / gross / sunig?
Do you have a flat for rent?	Händ Sii Wonig z'vermietä? (fr)
Do you know anybody who has a flat to rent?	Känned Sii öpper, wo ä Wonig z'vermietä hätt? (fr)
	Kännsch öpper, wo ä Wonig z'vermietä hätt? (inf)

BE AWARE!

Neighbours are usually quite friendly. You could engage in small talk using the different sections of this Survival Guide. Still, as it is common practice in Switzerland to share all the laundry facilities with them, in most cases the laundry room might be the only place you communicate with your neighbours.

Some Housing Words

Estate agency	Verwaltig (f)
Landlord	Vermieter (m)
	Vermieterin (f)
Tenant	Mieter (m)
	Mieterin (f)
One-room flat	Ainzimmerwonig (f)
Two-room flat	Zwaizimmerwonig (f)
Rental flat	Mietwonig (f)
Attic flat	Tachwonig (f)
	Attikawonig (f)
Neighbours	Nachbarä (pl)
Home owner	Huus-psizzer (m)
	Huus-psizzerin (f)
Two-level flat	Maisonette-Wonig (f) *(Mäsonet-Wonig)*

Laundry

Detergent	Wöschmittel (n)	**Laundry room**	Wöschchuchi (f)
to iron	büglä	**Laundry schedule**	Wöschplan (m)
Laundry basket	Zaine (f)	**Tumble drier**	Tumbler (m) *(Tömbler)*
Laundry	Wösch (f)	**washing**	wäschä
Laundry bag	Wöschsakk (m)	**Washing machine**	Wöschmaschine (f)
Laundry day	Wöschtag (m)		

Neighbourly Survival Phrases (formal)

Please close the door!	Bitte mached Sii d'Huustür zuä!
Where can I throw my rubbish?	Wo chann ich dä Apfall hiituä?
Could you please keep the noise down?	Chönd Sii bitte echli ruig Sii?
I'm trying to sleep.	Ich möcht schlafä.
Would you like to come over for a coffee?	Möchtet Sii mal zu ois zum Kafi cho?
I'm your new neighbour.	Ich bin Irä noi Nachbar. (m)
	Ich bin Iri noi Nachbarin. (f)

Housing

Estate Agent Survival Phrases (formal)

I have problems with my neighbours.	Ich ha Problem / Krach mit dä Nachbarä
The... is not working.	Dä…isch kaputt
Please, can you send a repairman?	Chönd Sii bitte än Handwerker pschtelä?
When are we signing the contract?	Wänn chömmer dä Vertrag underschriibä?
I will move in, in...	Ich will im…iiziä.
I will move out in…	Ich will im…uusziä.
We need to check the inventory.	Mir müänd no äs Abgabeprotokoll machä.
It was like that when I moved in.	So hätt's usgsee, wo mir iizogä sind.

Questions You May Ask Your Landlord (formal)

How much is the rent?	Wiä höch isch d'Mieti?
What services are included with the rent?	Was isch i dä Mieti inbegriffä?
Do you have a cellar / attic /...?	Händ Sii än Chäller / ä Windä...?
How much is a parking space per month?	Wiä vill choschtet än Parkplazz pro Monät?
How long is the cancellation period?	Wiä lang isch Kündigungsfrischt?
Where can I do my laundry?	Wo channi mini Wösch wäschä?
When can I do my laundry?	Wänn chann ich wäschä?
Are pets allowed?	Sind Huustier erlaubt?
How much is the deposit?	Wiä hoch isch d'Kauzion?
Is there a school / playground nearby?	Hätt's ä Schuäl / än Schpillplazz i dä Nöchi?
Are you planning to raise the rent?	Planned Sii, d'Mieti z'erhöchä?
Can I paint the walls?	Chann ich d'Zimmer schtrichä?
When was the house renovated?	Wänn isch das Huus renoviert wordä?
When can I move in?	Wänn chann ich iiziä?
Can I use the terrace / garden?	Törf ich d'Terrassä / dä Gartä benuzzä?
How far is it to the next bus station?	Wiä wiit isch äs bis zur nächschtä Bus-schtazion?

Housing

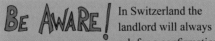 In Switzerland the landlord will always ask for a confirmation that you have a good credit standing:

Chann ich än Betribigsuuszug ha?
(May I have a clearance from the debt collection office?)

Questions Your Landlord May Ask You (formal)

Are you married?	Sind Sii verhüratet?
Do you have pets?	Händ Sii Huustier?
Yes, I have a dog / guinea pig.	Ja, ich ha än Hund / äs Meersoili.
Do you have a steady income?	Händ Sii än feschtä Loon?
How much do you earn?	Wiä vill verdiäned Sii?
I earn ... francs.	Ich verdiänä .... Frankä.
Do you have any children?	Händ Sii Chind?
How old are they?	Wiä alt sind diä?
Do you play an instrument?	Schpilled Sii äs Inschtrumänt?
Do you party a lot?	Mached Sii vill Partis?
Are you a foreigner?	Sind Sii Ussländer?
Where are you from?	Vo wo chömed Sii?
Have you ever been prosecuted?	Sind Sii je betribä wordä?
Do you smoke?	Rauched Sii?
Yes, I smoke.	Ja, ich rauchä.
No, I don't smoke.	Nai, ich rauchä nöd.

Numbers

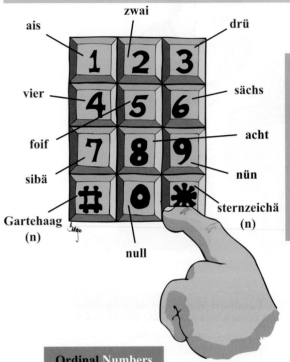

ais

zwai

drü

vier

sächs

acht

foif

nün

sibä

sternzeichä (n)

Gartehaag (n)

null

BE AWARE!

In Switzerland, digits are called **'Zalä'**. Number is **'Nummerä'** and refers to a set of digits, e.g. **Telefonnummerä** (phone number) or **Huusnummerä** (house number).

Ordinal Numbers

ten	zä	**fifty**	füfzg
eleven	elf	**sixty**	sächzg
twelve	zwölf	**seventy**	sibäzg
thirteen	drizä	**eighty**	achtzg
fourteen	vierzä	**ninety**	nünzg
fifteen	füfzä	**one hundred**	hundert
sixteen	sächzä	**two hundred**	zwaihundert
seventeen	sibzä	**one thousand**	tuusig
eighteen	achzä	**two thousand**	zwaituusig
nineteen	nünzä	**hundred thousand**	hunderttuusig
twenty	zwänzg	**one million**	Million (f)
thirty	drissg	**one billion**	Milliard (f)
forty	vierzg		

Cardinal Numbers

first	erscht
second	zwait
third	dritt
fourth	viert
fifth	foift
sixth	sächst
seventh	sibät
eighth	acht
ninth	nünt
tenth	zät

BE AWARE!

Numbers between 13 and 100 are always read from right to left (as in High German) so 21 is read **einäzwänzg** (one and twenty), 22 is **zwaiäzwänzg** (two and twenty), etc.

Don't you want to be a Millionaire...?

Other Numbers

even numbers	gradi Zaalä
odd numbers	ungradi Zaalä
Phone number	Telefonnummerä (f)
House number	Huusnummerä (f)
Insurance number	Versicherigsnummerä (f)
lucky number	Glükkszaal (f)
unlucky number	Unglükkszaal (f)
Code	Ghaimnummerä (f)
	Kod (m)
plus	und / plus
minus	minus
equals	isch glich/ git
Pension number	AHV *(Ahavau)*-Nummerä (f)

Miscellaneous

Toilets

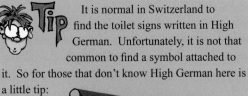

It is normal in Switzerland to find the toilet signs written in High German. Unfortunately, it is not that common to find a symbol attached to it. So for those that don't know High German here is a little tip:

Miscellaneous

Toilet Survival Phrases

Where is the toilet?	Wo isch s'WC *(Weze)*?
	Wo sind Toilettä *(Tualettä)*?
	Wo isch s'Hüüsli?
May I use your toilet?	Chann ich rasch uf d'Toilettä/
	uf s'WC?
Men's toilet	Mannätoilettä (pl)
Women's toilet	Frauätoilettä (pl)
Do you have any toilet paper?	Händ Sii WC-Papier? (fr)
	Häsch WC-Papier? (inf)
Where is the toilet light?	Wo ischs WC-Liächt?

Public Toilet Words

Toilet	Toilettä (f) *(Tualettä)*
	WC (n) *(Weze)*
Toilet paper	WC-Papier (n)
vacant	frei
engaged	psezt
Urinal	Pissoir (n) *(Pissuar)*
Washbasin	Lavabo (n) *(Lawabo)*
Soap	Soiffä (f)
Paper towel	Papiertuäch (n)
Hand dryer	Händtröchner (m)

Miscellaneous

Toilets in many public places are locked with a code system so that only the customers of the place can use them. On such occasions you can ask:

Wiä isch dä Kod für Toilettä / für's WC?
What is the code to open the toilet door?

General Non-Specific Terms

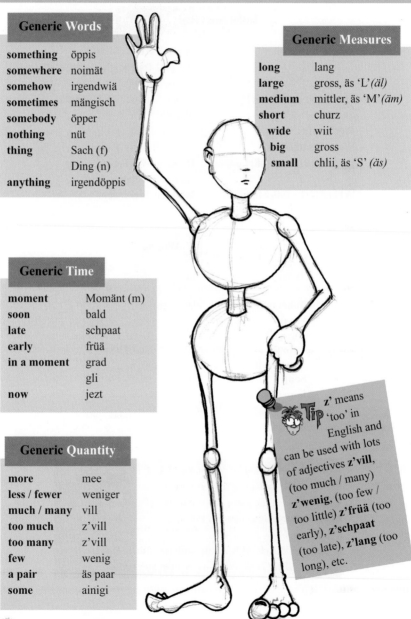

Generic Words

something	öppis
somewhere	noimät
somehow	irgendwiä
sometimes	mängisch
somebody	öpper
nothing	nüt
thing	Sach (f)
	Ding (n)
anything	irgendöppis

Generic Measures

long	lang
large	gross, äs 'L' (äl)
medium	mittler, äs 'M' (äm)
short	churz
wide	wiit
big	gross
small	chlii, äs 'S' (äs)

Generic Time

moment	Momänt (m)
soon	bald
late	schpaat
early	früä
in a moment	grad
	gli
now	jezt

Generic Quantity

more	mee
less / fewer	weniger
much / many	vill
too much	z'vill
too many	z'vill
few	wenig
a pair	äs paar
some	ainigi

Tip z' means 'too' in English and can be used with lots of adjectives **z'vill**, (too much / many) **z'wenig**, (too few / too little) **z'früä** (too early), **z'schpaat** (too late), **z'lang** (too long), etc.

Miscellaneous

Colours

hell   dunkel

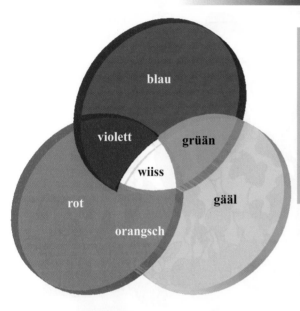

blau

violett   grüän

wiiss

rot   gääl

orangsch

schwarz   grau

The words **'hell'** (light) and **'dunkel'** (dark) can be put in front of most colours: **hellgrüän** (light green), **hellrot** (light red), **dunkelblau** (dark blue), **dunkelbruun** (dark brown)

Other Colours

pink	rosa
silver	silbrig
gold	goldig
brown	bruun
beige	beige
	(*bäsch*)
lilac	lila

 Swiss Expressions related to colours

green behind the ears	(immature)	grüän hinder dä Oorä
to have a green thumb	(to be good with plants)	än grüänä Tumä
to see it black	(to be pessimistic)	schwarz gsee
Black market	(illegal market)	Schwarzmärt (m)
a golden hand	(a lucky hand)	ä goldigi Hand
A white waistcoat	(innocent)	ä wiissi Weschtä
to be 'blue'	(to be drunk)	blau / er isch blau
A grey mouse	(a person that no one notices)	äs graus Müsli
to see things in pink clouds	(to be naïve)	dur ä rosaroti Brülä gsee

Miscellaneous

Animals

Fly
Flügä (f)

Bird
Vogel (m)

Horse
Ross (n)

Fish
Fisch (m)

Cow
Chuä (f)

Goat
Gaiss (f)

Pig
Sau (f)

Chicken
Huän (n)

Cat
Chazz (f)
Büsi (n)

Rabbit
Chüngel (m)

Dog
Hund (m)

Snake
Schlangä (f)

Miscellaneous

Alpine Wildlife

Marmot	Murmeli (n)	**Wild boar**	Wildsau (f)
	Murmeltiär (n)	**Lynx**	Luchs (m)
	Munggä (m)	**Wolf**	Wolf (m)
European ibex	Schtaibokk (m)	**Buzzard**	Moisebussard (m)
Eagle	Adler (m)	**Marten**	Marder (m)
Roe deer	Ree (n)	**Fox**	Fuchs (m)
Deer	Hirsch (m)	**Mouse**	Muus (f)/ Müsli (n)
Chamois	Gäms (f)	**Jackdaw**	Doolä (f)

Other Animals

Bear	Bär (m)
Bull	Schtiär (m)
Crocodile	Krokodil (n)
Donkey	Esel (m)
Elephant	Elefant (m)
Guinea pig	Meersoili (n)
Hippopotamus	Nilpferd (n)
	Flusspferd (n)
Lamb	Lamm (n)
Lion	Loi (m)
Lizard	Aidächsli (n)
Monkey	Aff (m)
Rhinoceros	Nashorn (n)
Rooster	Güggel (m)
Tiger	Tiger (m)
Turtle	Schildchrot (f)
Zebra	Zebra (n)

Miscellaneous

Bug	Wanzä (f)	**Slug**	Schnägg (m)	**Wasp**	Wäschpi (n)
Insect	Insekt (n)	**Spider**	Schpinä (f)	**Cockroach**	Kakerlakä (f)
Beetle	Chäfer (m)	**Worm**	Wurm (m)	**Ant**	Amaisä (f)
Fly	Flügä (f)	**Bee**	Biändli (n)		
Mosquito	Muggä (f)		Biänä (f)		

Bugs / Insects

Time

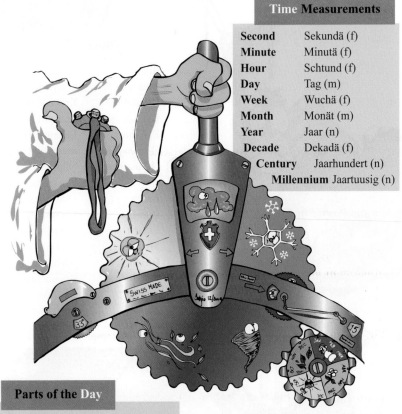

Miscellaneous

Time Measurements

Second	Sekundä (f)
Minute	Minutä (f)
Hour	Schtund (f)
Day	Tag (m)
Week	Wuchä (f)
Month	Monät (m)
Year	Jaar (n)
Decade	Dekadä (f)
Century	Jaarhundert (n)
Millennium	Jaartuusig (n)

Parts of the Day

Dawn	Dämmerig (f)
	Morgädämmerig (f)
Morning	Morgä (m)
Noon / Midday	Mittag (m)
Afternoon	Namittag (m)
Evening	Aabig (m)
Dusk	Dämmerig (f)
	Aabigdämmerig (f)
Night	Nacht (f)

The Seasons

Season	Jaaresziit (f)
Spring	Früälig (m)
Summer	Summer (m)
Autumn	Härpscht (m)
Winter	Winter (m)

Moments in Time

Past	vergangä
	Vergangähait (f)
Present / now	jezt
	Gägäwart (f)
Future	Zuäkumft (f)
	zuäkümftig
Yesterday	geschter
Today	hüt
Tomorrow	morn
Weekend	Wuchänänd (n)
the day before yesterday	vorgeschter
the day after tomorrow	übermorn

GRAMMAR

The answer to the question 'when' is 'am' for masculine and 'i dä' for feminine nouns: am Mittag (at noon), i dä Nacht (at night).

Key Survival Phrases

What time is it?	Wiä schpaat isch äs?
	Was isch für Ziit?
At what time...?	Wänn…?
When do we meet?	Wänn träffämmar ois?
When do you go to..?	Wänn gönd Sii uf..? (fr)
	Wänn gasch uf…? (inf)
Sorry, I am late.	Tuät mir Laid, ich bi z'schpaat
I will be 10 minutes late.	Ich chumä zä Minutä z'schpaat.
What day is today?	Welä Tag hämmer hüt?
	Was isch hüt für än Tag?
When is that?	Wänn isch das?
From when / until when?	Vo wänn / bis wänn?
exactly	genau
Do you have time?	Händ Sii Ziit? (fr)
	Häsch Ziit? (inf)
every week	jedi Wuchä
every month / every year	jedä Monät / jedäs Jaar
When does the film start?	Wänn fangt dä Film aa?
When does the film finish?	Wänn hört dä Film uf?
How long does the film last?	Wiä lang gat dä Film?
	Wiä lang durät dä Film?
The film starts at…	Dä Film fangt am … aa
The film finishes at…	Er hört am … uf

Miscellaneous

Days of the Week

Monday	Mäntig
Tuesday	Ziischtig
Wednesday	Mittwuch
Thursday	Dunnschtig
Friday	Friitig
Saturday	Samschtig
Sunday	Sunntig

Months of the Year

January	Januar (m)
February	Februar (m)
March	März (m)
April	April (m)
May	Mai (m)
June	Juni (m)
July	Juli (m)
August	Auguscht (m)
September	Septämber (m)
October	Oktober (m)
November	Novämber (m)
December	Dezämber (m)

GRAMMAR

All the months, days of the week and the seasons are masculine, which means that **dä** is used: **dä Januar, dä Mäntig, dä Früälig**).

To indicate time, the preposition **am** is used: **am drü**, means at three, **am sächsi** means at 6 o'clock.

Although most Swiss have a watch, sometimes you will be asked by strangers **'Händ Sii ä Uur?'** (Do you have a watch?). This question means: What time is it?

Miscellaneous

Telling Time

sächsi	föif ab sächsi	zä ab sächsi	Viertel ab sächsi	zwänzg ab sächsi

Föif vor halbi sibni (literarlly: 'five before half seven')	halbi sibni	föif ab halbi sibni (literally: 'five after half seven')

zwänzg vor sibni	Viertel vor sibni	zä vor sibni	föif vor sibni	sibni

Before **Vor** **Ab** After

Weather & Temperature

Key Survival Phrases

The sun is shining.	D'Sunä schiint.
It's raining.	Äs rägnät.
It's snowing.	Äs schnait.
It's chilly/foggy/humid.	Äs isch chüäl/näblig/füächt.
It's going to rain.	Äs chunnt go rägnä.
Today it's very warm / cold.	Hüt isch äs warm / chalt.
It's getting chilly.	Äs wird chüäl.
Summer is coming.	Dä Summer chunnt.
The weather is improving.	Äs tuät uf.
warm wind coming from the south	Föön (m) *(Foehn)*
What is the weather forecast for tomorrow?	Wiä isch dä Wätterpricht für morn?

BE AWARE! The 'weather verbs' (**rägnä, schneiä,** etc.) always need the impersonal subject **äs, äs rägnät** (it's raining).

Weather is the number one small-talk topic in Switzerland. It is often used as a topic to start a conversation.

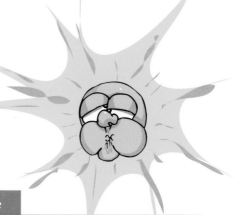

Weather & Temperature

Climate	Klima (n)	**Lightning**	Blizz (m)
cloudy	wolkig / bedekkt	**Rain**	Räge (m) / rägnä
sunny	sunig	**Snow**	Schnee (m)
cold	chalt	**Storm**	Schturm (m)
cool	chüel	**Sun**	Sunä (f)
dry	trochä	**Temperature**	Temperatur (f)
Fog	Näbel (m)	**Thunder**	Tunner (m)
Forecast	Wätterpricht (m)	**Thunderstorm**	Gwitter (n)
Hail	Hagel (m) / haglä	**warm**	warm
Heat	Hizz (f)	**Weather**	Wätter (n)
hot	haiss	**Weather report**	Wätterpricht (m)
humid	füecht	**Wind**	Wind (m)

Miscellaneous

Part III

Decoding the Swiss

117

Swiss 'Slanguage'

This last part of the Survival Guide presents some of the key Swiss German words and expressions which are often used in an informal environment. These are used by people of all social classes and ages, but it is the younger generation that may be found using the 'slanguage' more often.

The origin of the Swiss 'slanguage' varies: some words are typical Swiss words that have adopted a new meaning, metaphorical in some cases (**D'Ufzgi sind schoggi** – The homework is easy). Some other words are foreignisms, which means that the word is peculiar to a foreign language, but the grammatical pattern follows the Swiss German one. In particular the influence of the American and British culture, which is quite strong, plays an important role in younger people's words and expressions (foodä for eat).

As with fashion, Swiss words keep evolving and changing; the words used today could possibly change their spelling or meaning tomorrow. Because it is a 'moving target', it is advisable to keep track of the type of Swiss German the people around you are using, and try to adapt to it.

Slang Words (especially in Zurich)

A

än Abgang machä	to leave
Äs isch voll abgangä.	It was exciting.
abgspeist	remarkably good
abtanzä	to dance non-stop
achozzä	to be reluctant to do something
anderscht (mega)	very
aschissä	not in the mood for something

B

(inä)biigä	to eat
bö	no idea
brätschä	to drink
Buddle (f)	a bottle
büglä	to work hard

C

Chämi (n)	heavy smoker
Chazz(f)	attractive woman
chisä	to throw up
Chischtä (f)	a million francs
chluppä	to steal
chnüttlä	to work hard

D

deftig	great
derb	bad, disgusting (also: great, fantastic)

Continued on the next page...

Slang Words (especially in Zurich)

E

ebä	that's what I said, exactly
ee scho	OK, of course

F

fägä	to take great pleasure
filzä	to frisk, to shake down
foodä (fuudä)	to eat something
fridlich	peaceful, comfortable
Frittä (f)	hairstyle

G

gäch	great, brilliant
gedigä	comfortable

H

hängä / umehängä	to spend time somewhere or with someone
hammer	super
Hänger (m)	a lazy person
huerä	extremely

Huscheli (n) — a wall flower

J

jentschtes / jeni	a lot of something

K

voll krass	very cool
kuul	cool
än Knall ha	crazy

L

Lappä (m)	100 francs
Lungebröötli (n)	cigarette

M

mega	extremely, super
Mönggi (n)	idiot
muffä	to stink
muggä	to steal
müzzä	to sleep

Continued on the next page...

Slang Words (especially in Zurich)

P

plegerä	to relax
Primo (m)	primitive person
Puff (n)	disorder

S

scheikä	to dance
schiäf	odd, strange
schlotä	to smoke heavily
Schnügel (m)	nice looking guy
schoggi	easy
än Schönä	have a nice day/ evening
schpüälä	to forget, to fail
schräg	odd, strange
Schtuzz	money
(än mega) Schuss	attractive woman
smsle *(äsämäslä)*	to send an SMS to someone
so z'vill	superfluous
Suchthuufä (m)	person with addictive behaviour
suuffä	to drink a lot

T

Tonä (f)	1000 Swiss francs
tscheggä	to understand
tubä	to run away
Turi (m)	a tourist
tschillä	to cool off, to relax

U

us-tiggä	to go mad, to go crazy

V

verarschä	to cheat on somebody
verbokkä	fail
verbrächä	make a stupid mistake
verhäderet	confusing, entangled
verhängä	to forget
verhängt	missed (opportunity)
verhaizä	to mistreat
verhängtä Siäch	person who doesn't care about anything
(a Prüefig) verhauä	to fail (a test)
versiächä	to fail, to forget
versiffä	to miss out on something
voll edel	really nice, beautiful

W

waisch wo?	certainly not !
Was gaat ap?	What's up?

Z

Zäme!	Hi, guys !
ziä	buy, have a drink
zupfä	to leave

Swiss Idioms

Sayings and expressions are a key part of the linguistic heritage of a society. They are very interesting since they reflect, in a playful way, a lot about the social culture, and the Swiss are quite creative when it comes to using them.

As a final point, we would like to introduce some of these Swiss sayings and expressions. Comparing them with the ones used in other countries, one can find some similarities in the metaphorical meaning as well as with the expression itself; however, the majority of them are unique to Swiss German.

Swiss Idiom	Literal Translation	Meaning
Er isch uusgraschtet.	He freaked out.	He freaked out.
Sii hätt ä langi Laitig.	She has a long cable.	She is slow to catch the meaning.
ufs Gratwool	on the off chance	on the off chance
Da lit dä Hund begrabä.	That's where the dog is buried.	the crux of the matter
Das isch kais Honigschläkkä.	It's not a honey lick.	It's difficult.
nümmä alli Tassä im Schrank	not all cups in the cupboard / S/he's missing cups in his/her cupboard.	crazy
Sii isch rächt blauoigig.	She is blue-eyed.	She is naive.
Das isch kain Schläkk.	That's not a lick.	It's difficult.
s'hinterletscht	The last thing.	last thing possible / the worst thing
Er kännt nüt.	He doesn't know anything.	He goes for it despite the odds.
Sii/Er hätt alles gä.	S/he gave everything.	S/he put in a maximum of effort.
Er isch scharf uf sii.	He is hot on her.	He fancies her (sexually).
vo Tutä und Blasä kai Aanig	no idea about hooting nor blowing	Really naïve / uninformed
ufläsä	to scrape	to pick up
ä schpizzi Zungä	A pointed tongue	straight to the point
Er hätt's sii abgschleppt.	He towed her off.	He seduced her and took her home.

Swiss Idiom	Literal Translation	Meaning
Häsch än Knall?	Do you have a bang?	Are you crazy?
Bisch durä bi rot?	Have you crossed on the red?	Have you lost your mind?
Ais um s'ander wiä z'Paris.	One thing after another, just like in Paris	one thing after another
än Schprung i dä Schüsslä	a crack in the bowl	crazy
Gat's no!	No way!	For sure not!
Ämenä gschänktä Gaul luägt mär nöd is Muul.	Don't look a gift horse in the mouth.	If it's a gift, don't criticize it.

Swiss Idiom	Literal Translation	Meaning
ufglaisä	to rerail	initiate
Ich drukk dir dä Tumä.	I press my thumb for you.	I will be thinking of you / wish you good luck.
Diä / Dä chammer dä Buggel aberutschä.	S/he can slide down my hump.	I don't care at all about her/him.
Sii / Er macht kain Wank.	S/he doesn't move.	S/he doesn't move or make a sound.
Hans was Hairi.	John is like Henry.	It's all the same.
Sii / Er macht d'Fuscht im Sakk.	S/he makes her/his fist in the pocket.	S/he is secretly angry.
Cervelat-Promi	sausage VIP Starlet	a would-like-to-be famous person
Schikki-Mikki	chic person	posh person
Sii haltet zäme wiä Päch und Schwefel.	They stick together like pitch and sulphur.	They are inseparable friends.
Sii / Er faart voll uf das ab.	S/he drives completely after this.	S/he is very much into this.
Sii / Er wott dä Foifer und s'Weggli.	S/he wants the penny and the roll.	S/he wants everything.
Sii / Er schwümmt im Gäld.	S/he is swimming in money.	S/he is very rich.
schaffä wiä än Tubel	work like a madman	work a lot
än Chazzäschprung	only a cat jump	only a few blocks away
Jezt chumm ich drus.	I'm coming out.	Now I understand.
wiä äs Lama	just like a lama	very slow

Appendix

Pronouns and Articles

Personal Pronouns

	1st person	2nd person	3rd person
nom, sg.	ich	du	er
acc. sg.	mich	di	in
dat. sg.	mir	dir	im
nom. pl.	mir	ier	sii
acc. pl.	ois	oi	sii
dat. pl,	ois	oi	inä

Definite Articles

	masculine	feminine	neuter	plural
common case	dä	d, di	s	d, di
dative case	äm	där	äm	dä

Indefinite Articles

	masculine	feminine	neuter
common case	än	ä	äs
dative case	ämä (n), ämänä(n)	ärä(n), änärä(n)	ämä(n), ämänä(n)

Demonstrative Pronouns

	masculine	feminine	neuter	plural
common case	dä	die	das	die
	desäb	disäb	säb	disäbe
dative case	däm	däre	däm	däne
	säbem	säbere	säbem	säbe
	emsäbe(n)	dersäbe	emsäbe	desäbe

Possessive Pronouns

	masculine	feminine	neuter	plural
common case	min	mini	mis	mini
dative case	mim	minärä	mim	minä
common case	din	dinerä	dis	dini
dative case	dim	dinerä	dim	dinä
common case	sin	sinä	sis	sini
dative case	sim	sinerä	sim	sinä
common case	oise(n)	oisä	oisäs	oisi
dative case	oisem	oisere	oisem	oise
common case	oie(n)	oii	oies	oii
dative case	oisem	oiere	oiem	oie(n)
common case	ire(n)	iri	ires	iri
dative case	irem	irärä	iräm	irä

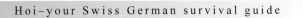

Verbs

Survival Verbs

	inf.	ich	du	er	mir	ier	sii
be	si	bi	bisch	isch	sind	sind	sind
become	werde	wird	wirsch	wird	wärded	wärded	wärded
come	cho	chumm	chunsch	chunnt	chömmed	chömmed	chömmed
do	tuä	tuä	tuäsch	tuät	tüänd	tüänd	tüänd
drink	trinkä	trinkä	trinksch	trinkt	drinked	drinked	drinked
drive	faarä	faarä	faarsch	faart	faaret	faaret	faaret
eat	ässä	ässä	issisch	isst	ässed	ässed	ässed
give	ge	gibä	gisch	git	gänd	gänd	gänd
go	gaa	gang	gasch	gat	gönd	gönd	gönd
have	ha	ha	häsch	hätt	händ	händ	händ
hear	losä	losä	losisch	losed	losed	losed	losed
hold	hebä	hebä	hebsch	hebt	hebed	hebed	hebed
like	gärn ha	ha gärn	häsch gärn	er hät gärn	händ gärn	händ gärn	händ gärn
love	liäbä	liäbä	liäbsch	liäbt	liäbed	liäbed	liäbed
say	sägä	sägä	säisch	säit	säged	säged	säged
see	luägä	luägä	luägsch	luägt	luäged	luäged	luäged
sleep	schlafä	schlafä	schlafsch	schlaft	schlafed	schlafed	schlafed
travel	raisä	raisä	raisisch	raist	raised	raised	raised
walk	lauffä	lauffä	lauffsch	laufft	lauffed	lauffed	lauffed
want	welä	will	willsch	will	wännd	wännd	wännd
wash	wäschä	wäschä	wäschisch	wäsched	wäsched	wäsched	wäsched
work	schaffä	schaffä	schaffisch	schafft	schaffed	schaffed	schaffed

Other Common Past Tenses (Perfect tense)

Ich bi gsi	**I have been / I was**
Ich ha gmacht	**I have made / I made**
Ich ha trunkä	**I have drunk / I drank**
Ich ha gässä	**I have eaten / I ate**
Ich ha gschlafä	**I have slept / I slept**
Ich bi gloffä	**I have walked / I walked**
Ich bi gangä	**I have gone / I went**
Ich ha glosed	**I have listened / I listened**
Ich ha gschaffed	**I have worked / I worked**
Ich bi gfaarä	**I have driven / I drove**
I ha gluäged	**I have watched / I watched**

BE AWARE!

There is neither a simple past nor a past perfect in Swiss German.

The past in German is built with the verb **ha** (have) + the past participle:
Ich ha d'Ufzgi gmacht (I did my homework).

Some verbs (usually movements) build the past with the verb **si** (to be) + the past participle:
Ich bin uf Züri gangä (I went to Zurich).

Modal Verbs

	Inf	1 pres	2 pres	pl. pres	subj.	cond.
can	chönä	cha	chasch	chönd	chönn	chönd
like	mögä	mag	magsch	möge	mög	möcht
may	törffä	törff	törfsch	törffed	törffi	törft
must	müäsä	müäs, müän	müäsch	müänd	müäs	müässt
should	sölä	söll	sölsch	söled	söll	sött
want	welä	wott, will	wotsch	wänd	well	wett

The Dictionary
English to Swiss German
Swiss German to English

Dictionary

English
to
Swiss German

A

English	Swiss German
Abdomen	Buuch (m)
above (prep)	über
Abscess	Apszäss (m)
according to (prep)	nach
across (prep)	über
across from (prep)	gägänüber
Address	Adrässä (f)
Address book	Addrässbuäch (n)
Adult	Erwachsenä/i (m/f)
Advertising	Wärbig (f)
Aeroplane	Flugzüg (n)
afraid	ängschtlich
after (prep)	nach
Afternoon	Namittag (m)
against (prep)	gägä
Airmail	Luftposcht (f)
allergic to	alergisch gägä
Allergy	Alergii (f)
along (prep)	entlang
Alpenhorn	Alphorn (m)
amazed	erschtunt
Ambulance	Ambulanz (f)
Ambulance	Chrankäwagä (m)
angry	bös
Ankle	Chnöchel (m)
Answering machine	Telefonbeantworter(m)
Ant	Amaisä (f)
Antidote	Gägägift (n)
anxious	ängschtlich
anything	irgendöppis
Appendicitis	Blinddarmenzündig (f)
Appetizer	Aperitif (m)
Appetizer	Apero (m)
Apple	Öpfel (m)
Apple juice	Öpfelsaft (m)
Apple juice	Süässmoscht (m)
Appointment	Termin (m)
Appraisal	Quali(fikation) (f)
Appraisal	Laischtigsbewärtig (f)
Apprentice	Leerling (m)
April	April (m)
Area code	Vorwaal (f)
argue (verb)	schtriitä
Argument	Schtriit (m)
Arm	Arm (m)

English	Swiss German
around (prep)	um
Arrival	Akunft (f)
Article	Artikel (m)
Art	Kunscht (f)
Aspirin	Aschpirin (n)
Assistant	Asischtänt/in (m/f)
Asthma	Aschtma (n)
at (prep)	bi
at (prep)	am
Attachment	Attachment (n)
	(Attätschmänt)
Attic	Eschtrich (m)
Attic	Windä (f)
Attic flat	Tachwonig (f)
Attic flat	Attikawonig (f)
August	Auguscht (m)
Aunt	Tantä (f)
Autumn	Härpscht (m)
Avalanche	Lawinä (f)

B

B&B	B&B (n)
Baby boy	Büäbli (n)
Baby girl	Maitli (n)
Back	Ruggä (m)
Bacon	Schpäkk (m)
bad	schlächt
bad luck	Päch (n)
Baguette	Pariserbrot (n)
Bakery	Bekk (m)
Bakery	Bekkerei (f)
Balcony	Balkon (m)
Banana	Bananä (f)
Bandage	Verband (m)
Band-aid	Pfläschterli (n)
Bank	Bank (f)
Bank account	Bankkonto (n)
Banknotes	Banknotä (f)
Bar	Bar (f)
Barbecue	Grillfäscht (n)
Basement	Undergschoss (n)
Basement garage	Tüfgarasch (f)
Bath tub	Badwannä (f)
Bathroom	Badzimmer (n)
Beach	Schtrand (m)
Beans	Boonä (f)
Bear	Bär (m)
beautiful	schön
Bed	Bett (n)
Bed cover	Bettazug (m)
Bedroom	Schlafzimmer (n)
Bee	Biändli (n)
Bee	Biinä (f)
Beef	Rindflaisch (n)
Beer	Biär (n)
Beetle	Chäfer (m)
behind (prep)	hinder
beige	beige (bäsch)
Bellybutton	Buchnabel (m)
Belt	Gürtel (m)
Belt	Gurt (m)

English	Swiss German
beneath (prep)	under
beside (prep)	näbäd
between (prep)	zwüschä
big	gross
billion	Milliard (f)
Bird	Vogel (m)
Birthday party	Geburtstags-party (f)
bitter	bitter
black	schwarz
blink (verb)	blinzlä
Blood	Bluät (n)
Blood pressure	Bluätdrukk (m)
Blood sugar	Bluätzukker (m)
Blouse	Blusä (f)
blow (verb)	blasä
blue	blau
Board of Directors	Verwaltigsrat (m)
Body lotion	Körperlozioon (f)
boiled	gkocht
Bonus	Bonus (m)
Book	Buäch (n)
Book shelves	Büächergschtell (n)
Bookshop	Buächhandlig (f)
Bookshop	Büächerladä (m)
Border	Gränzä (f)
bored	glangwiilet
Boss	Chef/in (m/f)
	(Schef/in)
Bottom	Füdli (n)
Bowl	Schüsslä (f)
Box	Schachtlä (f)
Box	Chischtä (f)
Boy	Buäb (m)
Bra	Beha (m)
Brand	Markä (f)
Bread	Brot (n)
Break	Pausä (f)
Breakfast	Zmorgä (m)
Breast	Busä (m)
Bridge	Brugg (f)
Briefcase	Arbetsmappä (f)
Broccoli	Broggoli (m)
Broken bone	Chnochäbruch (m)
Brother	Brüäder (m)
Brother-in-law	Schwager (m)
brown	bruun
brown bread	dunkels Brot (n)
Brunch	Brunch (m)
Brush	Bürschtä (f)
Bug	Wanzä (f)
Building	Geboide (n)
Building (new)	Noibau (m)
Bull	Schtiär (m)
Bulletin board	Aschlagbrätt (n)
Bunker	Luftschuzzchäller (m)
burn (verb)	verbränä
burp (verb)	görpsä
burp (verb)	görpslä (Babys)
Bus	Bus (m)
Bus station	Busbaanhof (m)
Bus stop	Bushalteschtell (f)
Bus ticket	Busbilet (n)

Dictionary

134

Business casual	unzwungä	Chicken	Büsi (n)
Butcher's shop	Mezzg (f)	Children's room	Chinderzimmer (n)
Butter	Butter (m)	Chimney	Chämi
Butter	Ankä (m)	Church	Chilä (f)
Button	Chnopf (m)	Cider	suurä Moscht (m)
buy (verb)	poschtä	Cigarette	Lungebröötli (n)
buy (verb)	chauffä		(slang)
Buzzard	Moisebussard (m)	Cinema	Kino (n)
by (prep)	bi	City	Schtadt(f)
by (prep)	bis	City	City (f) *(Sitti)*
by (transp) (prep)	mit	City map	Schtadtplan (m)
Bye	Uf widerluägä	Cleaner	Puzzma/frau (m/f)
Bye	Uf widersee!	Climate	Klima (n)
Bye	adieu *(Adjö)*	Clinic	Klinik (f)
Bye (informal)	ciao *(tschau)*	Closet	Chaschtä (m)
Bye (informal)	Tschüss	Clothing	Chlaider (pl)
		cloudy	wolkig
C		cloudy	bedekkt
		Coat	Mantel (m)
Cable TV	Kabelfernse (n)	Cockroach	Kakerlakä (f)
Cake	Chuächä (m)	Code (secret)	Ghaimnummerä (f)
cancel (verb)	löschä	Code	Kod (m)
cancel (verb)	känslä	Coffee bar / cafe	Kafi (n)
Candy	Zältli (n)	Coffee break	Kafipausä (f)
Canteen	Mensa (f)	Coffee party	Kafiklatsch (m)
Canteen	Kantinä (f)	Coffee party	Kafichränzli (n)
Cap	Chappä (f)	Coffee with cream	Kafi (crème) (m)
Cappuccino	Cappuccino (m)	Coffee with milk	Milchkafi (m)
	(Gaputschino)	Coffee with milk	Schalä (f)
Car	Auto (n)	Coin	Münzä (f)
Care of	zuhandä vo	Coke	Coggi (n)
careful	Achtung	Cold	Vercheltig (f)
Carnival	Fasnacht (f)	cold	chalt
Carpet	Teppich (m)	cold chocolate	chalti Schoggi (f)
Carrots	Rüäbli (n)	cold drinks	chalti Getränk (pl)
Cash	Cash *(Käsch)*	Collar	Chragä (m)
Cash	Bargäld (n)	Colleague	Arbetskolleg/in (m/f)
Cash machine	Gäldautomat (m)	collect (verb)	sammlä
Cashier	Kassierer/in (m/f)	Comb	Schträäl (m)
Cat	Chazz (f)	comfortable	gedigä (slang)
Cathedral	Katedraale (f)	Commission	Komission (f)
Cauliflower	Bluämächöl (m)	complain (verb)	mozzä (slang)
Celebrity	Promi (m)	Concert	Konzärt (n)
Celebrity	VIP (m) *(Wiaipi)*	Concierge	Consierge (m)
Cellar	Chäller (m)		*(Gonsiersch)*
Century	Jaarhundert (n)	Concussion	Ghirnerschütterig (f)
Chair	Schtuäl (m)	Condiment	Aromat (n)
Chamois	Gäms (f)	Condiment	Gwürz (pl)
Change (money)	Münz (n)	Condom	Kondom (n)
Channel	Kanal (m)	Conference	Konfäränz (f)
check in (verb)	iitschäggä	Connection	Verbindig (f)
check out (verb)	uus-tschäggä	Consultant	Berater/in (m/f)
Cheek	Baggä (m)	contagious	aschtekkänd
cheerful	fröölich	Continent	Kontinänt (m)
Cheers	Proscht	Contract	Vertrag (m)
Cheers	Pröschtli	Contraceptive	Verhüetigsmittel (n)
Cheese	Chäs (m)	cool	cool (kuul)
Cheque	Schegg (m)	cool (temperature)	chüel
Cherry	Chriäsi (m)	copy (verb)	kopierä
Chest	Bruscht (f)	Corn	Mais (m)
Chicken	Huän (n)	Corner	Eggä (m)
Chicken	Poulet (n) *(Pule)*	Corn on the cob	Mais-cholbä (m)

Costs	Choschtä (pl)
cosy	haimelig
cosy	gmüätlich
Cotton	Baumwule (f)
cough (verb)	huäschtä
Counter	Schalter (m)
Country	Land (n)
County	Kanton (m)
Course	Kurs (m)
Cousin	Cousine (f) *(Gusinä)*
Cousin	Cousin (m) *(Gusän)*
cover (verb)	zuähebä
Cow	Chuä (f)
Crab	Krabä (f)
Cramp	Chrampf (m)
crazy	verrukkt
crazy	gaga
crazy	irr
Cream	Raam (m)
Cream	Crème (f) *(Gräm)*
Credit card	Kreditchartä (f)
Crocodile	Krokodil (n)
Croissant	Gipfeli (n)
Crossbow (shooting)	Armbruscht (schüssä)
Crossing	Chrüüzig (f)
cry (verb)	brüälä
cry (verb)	hüüla
Culture	Kultur (f)
Cup	Tassä (f)
Curd cheese	Quark (m)
Currency	Wäärig (f)
Curtains	Vorhäng (pl)
Customer	Chund/in (m/f)
Customs	Zoll (m)
Cutlery	Pschtekk (n)
D	
dance (verb)	tanzä
dark	dunkel
date (verb)	deitä
Daughter	Tochter (f)
Daughter-in-law	Schwigertochter (f)
Dawn	Dämmerig (f)
Dawn	Morgädämmerig (f)
Day	Tag (m)
Debit card	EC-Chartä (f)
	(Eze-Chartä)
Decade	Dekadä (f)
December	Dezämber (m)
declare (verb)	verzollä
deep fried	frittiert
Deer	Hirsch (m)
Delay	Verschpötig (f)
Deli (katessen)	Delikatessladä (m)
Deodorant	Deo (m)
Department	Aptailig (f)
Departure	Abrais (f)
Deposit (money)	Depot (n) *(Depo)*
Deposit (money)	Hinderlegig (f)
depressed	depressiv
Desk	Pult (n)

Desktop	Desktop (m)	**eighty**	achtzg	**Fingernail**	Fingernagel (m)
desperate	verzwiiflet	**Elbow**	Eläbogä (m)	**Fire**	Füür (n)
Dessert	Dessert (m)	**Electrical shop**	Elektrogschäft (n)	**Fireplace**	Cheminée (n)
Detergent	Wöschmittel (n)	**Elephant**	Elefant (m)		*(Schminee)*
Diabetes	Diabetis (f)	**eleven**	elf	**first**	erscht
diabetic	diabetisch	**Emergency**	Notfall (m)	**First Aid**	Erschti Hilf (f)
Diarrhoea	Durchfall (m)	**Emergency room**	Notufnaam (f)	**first floor**	erschtä Schtokk
Diet	Diät (f)	**emigrate (verb)**	uusraisä	**Fish**	Fisch (m)
Digestive	Vertailer (m)	**Employee**	Agschtellte (m)	**fish (verb)**	fischä
Digestive	Digestive (m)	**Employee**	Agschtellti (f)	**fish (verb)**	anglä
	(Dischestiv)	**Employer**	Arbetgeber/in (m/f)	**Fitness**	Fitness
Dining car	Schpiiswagä (m)	**engaged**	psezt	**five**	föif
Dining room	Ässzimmer (n)	**engaged**	verlobt	**Flag**	Faanä (f)
Dinner	Znacht (m)	**Entertainment**	Unterhaltig (f)	**Flavour**	Gschmakk (m)
Dinner	Znachtassä (n)	**Entrance**	Iigang (m)	**Floor**	Bodä (m)
Dinner service	Tischset (n)	**Entry way**	Iigangshallä (f)	**Flour**	Määl (n)
Director	Diräktor/in (m/f)	**Envelope**	Couvert (n) *(Kuwäär)*	**Flu**	Grippe (f)
disappointed	enttüscht	**envious**	niidisch	**Fly**	Flügä (f)
Discotheque	Disco (f)	**equals**	isch glich	**Foehn**	Föön (m)
discount	reduziert	**equals**	git	**Fog**	Näbel (m)
Discounts	Verbilligung (f)	**Estate agency**	Verwaltig (f)	**fold (verb)**	faltä
Dishes	Gschirr (n)	**European ibex**	Schtaibokk (m)	**Foot**	Fuäss (m)
Dishwasher	Abwäschmaschine (f)	**even numbers**	gradi Zaalä	**Footpath**	Wäg (m)
divorced	gschidä	**Evening**	Aabig (m)	**for (prep)**	für
Doctor	Arzt/(m) / Ärztin (f)	**Evening dress**	Aabigchlaid (n)	**Forecast**	Wätterpricht (m)
Doctor's surgery	Praxis (f)	**Event**	Event (m) *(iwent)*	**Forehead**	Schtirn (f)
Dog	Hund (m)	**Event**	Aalass (m)	**Foreigner**	Ussländer/in (m/f)
Donkey	Esel (m)	**Exchange rate**	Wächselratä (f)	**Forest**	Wald (m)
Door	Tüür (f)	**excited**	uufgreggt	**Fork**	Gablä (f)
Doorbell	Huusgloggä (f)	**Excuse me**	entschuldigung	**Form**	Formular (n)
Double bed	Doppelbett (n)	**Excuse me**	exgüsi	**forty**	vierzg
down	abä	**expensive**	tüür	**forward (verb)**	forwardä
Draft beer	Schtangä (f)	**Exposition**	Uus-schtellig (f)	**forward (verb)**	wiiterlaitä
Drawer	Schubladä (f)	**Expresso**	Espresso (m)	**four**	vier
Dress (noun)	Chlaid (n)	**Eye**	Aug (n)	**fourteen**	vierzä
dress (verb)	aaziiä	**Eyebrow**	Augebrauä (f)	**fourth**	viert
Dress code	Chlaidervorschrift (f)	**Eyelash**	Wimperä (pl)	**Fox**	Fuchs (m)
dressed	aazogä			**Freckles**	Märzetüpfli (pl)
Dressing	Salatsossä (f)	**F**		**Freezer**	Tüfchüäler (m)
Driver's licence	Faaruuswis (m)			**fresh**	früsch
Driver's licence	Bilet (n)	**Face**	Gsicht (n)	**Friday**	Friitig
Drops	Tröpfli (pl)	**Family get-together**	Familiäzämakunft (f)	**Fridge**	Chüälschrank (m)
drunk	blau (slang)	**Family get-together**	Familiäschluuch (m)	**fried**	prötlet
dry	trochä	**famous**	beründamt / bekannt	**Friend**	Fründ/in (m/f)
dry out (verb)	uuströchnä	**fantastic**	fantastisch	**from (prep)**	us
Dusk	Dämmerig (f)	**Farewell party**	Apschidsfäscht (n)	**from (prep)**	vo
Dusk	Aabigdämmerig (f)	**Fashion**	Modä (f)	**Frontier**	Gränzä (f)
Duvet	Bettdekki (f)	**Father**	Vatter (m)	**frozen**	tüfgfrorä
		Father -in-law	Schwigervatter (m)	**Fruit**	Frucht (f)
E		**Faucet/ tap**	Haanä (m)	**Frying pan**	Bratpfanä (f)
		February	Februar (m)	**Full board**	Vollpension (f)
Eagle	Adler (m)	**Fee**	Gebür (f)	**Full time**	vollziit
Ear	Oor (n)	**Fee**	Priis (m)	**funny**	luschtig
early	früä	**Fever**	Fiäber (n)	**funny**	wizzig
earn money	Gäld verdiänä	**few**	wenig	**furious**	hässig
eat (verb)	biigä (slang)	**Fiancé**	Verlobtä (m)	**Future**	Zuäkumft (f)
Editor	Herusgeber/in (m/f)	**Fiancée**	Verlobti (f)	**Future**	zuäkümftig
Egg	Ai (n)	**Field**	Fäld (n)		
Eggplant	Oberschinä (f)	**fifteen**	füfzä	**G**	
eight	acht	**fifth**	füft		
eighteen	achzä	**fifty**	füfzg	**gamble (verb)**	schpilä
eighth	acht	**Finger**	Finger (m)	**gamble (verb)**	gämblä

Dictionary

Game	Schpiil (n)	Headlines	Schlagzilä (pl)	into (prep)	gägä
Garage	Garage (f) *(Garasch)*	hear (verb)	ghörä	into (prep)	in
Garden	Gartä (m)	Heart	Härz (n)	invest money	Gäld inweschtierä
Garlic	Chnobli (m)	Heat	Hizz (f)	Investment	Inweschtizion (f)
Garlic	Chnoblauch (m)	Hello	Grüezi	Investment	Inweschtierig (f)
gay	schwul	Help	Hilfe (f)	Invoice	Rächnig (f)
Geography	Geografii (f)	Hen night	Polteraabig (m)	Iron	Bügälisä (n)
Girl	Maitli (n)	here	da	Island	Inslä (f)
Glass	Glas (n)	heterosexual	hetero(sexuell)		
Gloves	Häntschä (pl)	Hi (informal)	Hoi	**J**	
Goat	Gaiss (f)	Hi (informal)	Sali		
gold (colour)	gold	Hi (informal)	Salü	Jack salmon	Zander (m)
good	guet	Hi (to several)	Hoi zäme	Jackdaw	Doolä (f)
Goose bumps	Huänerhuut (f)	Highway	Autobaan (f)	Jacket	Jagge (f)
Gossip	Klatsch (m)	Hill	Hügel (m)	Jam	Gomfi (f)
Gossip	Tratsch (m)	Hip	Hüft (f)	Jam doughnut	Berliner (m)
gossip (verb)	klatschä	Hippopotamus	Flusspferd (n)	January	Januar (m)
grab (verb)	griiffä	Hippopotamus	Nilpferd (n)	jealous	ifersüchtig
grab (verb)	feschthebä	hold (verb)	hebä	Jeans	Jeans (pl) *(Tschins)*
Grandchild	Gros-chind (n)	homosexual	homo(sexuell)	Job application	Bewärbig (f)
Granddaughter	Änkelin (f)	Honey	Honig (m)	Job description	Jobbeschribig (f)
Grandfather	Grosvatter (m)	horny	schpizz	Job interview	Bewärbigsgschpräch(n)
Grandmother	Grosmuetter (f)	horny	giggerig	Joke	Wizz (m)
Grandparents	Groselterä (pl)	Horse	Ross (n)	joyful	froo
Grandson	Änkel (m)	Hospital	Schpital (n)	joyful	zfridä
Grapefruit juice	Grapefruitsaft (m)	hot	haiss	Juice	Saft (m)
	(Gräpfrüsaft)	hot chocolate	haissi Schoggi (f)	July	Juli (m)
Grape juice	Truubesaft (m)	hot milk	haissi Milch (f)	jump (verb)	gumpä
grateful	dankbar	hot wine	Glüäwii (m)	June	Juni (m)
Great aunt	Grostantä (f)	Hour	Schtund (f)		
Great grandfather	Urgrosvatter (m)	House number	Huusnummerä (f)	**K**	
Great grandmother	Urgrosmuetter (f)	Housewarming	Husiweiigs-party (f)		
Great uncle	Grosunggle (m)	How?	Wiä?	Key	Schlüssel (m)
green	grüän	hug (verb)	umarmä	kiss (verb)	küssä
grey	grau	humid	füecht	Kitchen	Chuchi (f)
Grill	Grill (m)	Humour	Humoor (m)	Kitchen shelves	Chuchiablagä (pl)
grilled	griliert	hundred	hundert	Knee	Chnü (n)
Groceries	Läbesmittel (pl)	hungry	Hunger (m)	Knife	Mässer (n)
Ground floor	Partär (n)	hurry	schnäll	kosher	koscher
Guinea pig	Meersoili (n)	Husband	Maa (m)		
Gutters	Tachrinnä (f)			**L**	
Gym	Fitnessruum (m)	**I**			
				Laboratory	Labor (n)
H		Ice cream	Glacé (n) *(Glasse)*	Lake	See (m)
		Iced tea	Iis-tee (m)	Lamb	Lamm (n)
Hail	Hagel (m)	Idiot	Mönggi (n) (slang)	land (verb)	landä
hail (verb)	haglä	immigrate (verb)	iiraisä	Landlord	Vermieter/in (m/f)
Hair	Haar (pl)	in (prep)	in	Laptop	Laptop (m) *(Läptop)*
halal	halal	in front of (prep)	vor	large	gross
Half board	Halbpension (f)	Income	Iikomä (n)	late	schpaat
Hallway	Gang (m)	Infection	Enzündig (f)	Latte Macchiato	Latte Macchiato (f)
Ham	Schinkä (m)	Injection	Schprüzzä (f)		*(Maggiato)*
Hand	Hand (f)	Injury	Verlezzig (f)	laugh (verb)	lachä
Hand cream	Handcreme (f)	Insect	Insekt (n)	Laundry	Wösch (f)
	(Handgräm)	Insomnia	Schlaflosikait (f)	Laundry bag	Wöschsakk (m)
Hand dryer	Händtröchner (m)	Insurance	Versicherig (f)	Laundry basket	Zaine (f)
Hanger	Chlaiderbügel (m)	Insurance number	Versicherigs-	Laundry day	Wöschtag (m)
happy	glükklich		nummerä (f)	Laundry room	Wöschchuchi (f)
Hat	Huät (m)	Intensive care	Intensivschtazion (f)	Laundry schedule	Wöschplan (m)
Hay fever	Hoischnuppä (m)	Interest	Zins (m)	Lawn	Rasä (m)
Head	Chopf (m)	International news	Ussland-Nachrichtä	Lawnmower	Rasämäier (m)
Headache	Chopfwee (n)		(pl)	Leather	Läder (n)

leave (verb)	abfaarä	Margarine	Margerinä (f)	next to (prep)	näbäd
left	linggs	marinated	mariniert	Niece	Nichtä (f)
Leg	Bai (n)	Marital status	Familiäschtand (m)	Night	Nacht (f)
Legumes	Hülsäfrücht (pl)	Marmalade	Orangschägomfi (f)	nine	nün
Lemon	Zitrone (f)	Marmot	Murmeli (n)	nineteen	nünzä
Lentils	Linsä (pl)	Marmot	Mumeltiär (n)	ninety	nünzg
lesbian	lesbisch	Marriage	Ehe (f)	ninth	nünt
less	weniger	married	verhüratet	Nipple	Bruschtwarzä (f)
Letter	Briäf (m)	Marten	Marder (m)	no	nai
Lettuce	Chopfsalat (m)	Massage	Massage (f) (Masaasch)	Noon/ midday	Mittag (m)
Library	Bibliothek (f)	May	Mai (m)	Nose	Nasä (f)
lick (verb)	lutschä	Meals	Maalzitä (pl)	nothing	nüt
Lift	Lift (m)	Meat	Flaisch (n)	November	Novämber (m)
light (colour)	hell	Medicine	Hailmittel (n)	now	jezt
Lightning	Blizz (m)	medium (size)	mittleri Grössi	Nurse	Chrankäschwöschter (f)
Lilac	lila	medium (size)	äs M	Nurse	Pflägfachfrau/maa (f/m)
Lime	Limone (f)	medium (meat)	halb durä	Nylon	Nylon (n) (Nailon)
Linen	Liinä (f)	Meeting	Beschprächig (f)		
Lion	Loi (m)	Meeting	Sizzig (f)	O	
listen (verb)	losä	Microwave	Mikrowälä (f)		
Liver	Läbere (f)	mild	mild	Obituary	Todesaazaig (f)
Lizard	Aidächsli (n)	Milk	Milch (f)	Occupation	Job (m) (Tschop)
Loan	Darleä (n)	milk (verb)	mälchä	Occupation	Pruäf (m)
Lobby	Vorhallä (f)	Millennium	Jaartuusig (n)	Ocean	Ozean (m)
Lobby	Vorruum (m)	million	Million (f)	October	Oktober (m)
Lobster	Hummer (m)	Mineral water	Mineralwasser (n)	odd numbers	ungradi Zaalä
Local call	lokale Aaruäf (m)	minus	minus	of (prep)	vo
Local news	lokali Noiigkaitä (pl)	Minute	Minutä (f)	Office	Gschäft (n)
Local news	lokali Nachrichtä (pl)	Minutes	Protokoll (n)	Office	Büro (n)
log in (verb)	iiloggä	Mirror	Schpiägel (m)	old building	Altbau (m)
log out (verb)	uusloggä	Mobile phone	Händi(n)	old man	altä Maa
lonely	ainsam	Mobile phone	Natel (n)	old woman	alti Frau
long	lang	moment	Momänt (m)	Olive oil	Olivenöl (n)
long distance call	internazionalä Aaruäf (m)	Monday	Mäntig	on (hor. surfaces)	uf
long sleeves	langärmlig	Money	Gäld (m)	on (ver. surfaces)	a(m)
long-sighted	wiitsichtig	Monkey	Aff (m)	one	äis
look (verb)	luägä	Month	Monät (m)	one thousand	(ain)-tuusig
Loss	Verluscht (m)	more	mee	One-room apt.	Aizimmerwonig (f)
Lounge	Schtubä (f)	Morning	Morgä (m)	Onion	Zwiblä (f)
love (verb)	liäbä	Mosque	Moschee (f)	Onion	Bölä (pl)
lovely	härzig	Mosquito	Muggä (f)	Opera	Operä (f)
lucky number	Glükkszaal (f)	Mother	Muetter (f)	Operation	Operazion (f)
Luggage	Gepäkk (n)	Mother-in-law	Schwigermuetter (f)	Operator	Vermittlig (f)
Lunch	Zmittagässä (n)	Mountain	Bärg (m)	Opinion	Mainig (f)
Lunch	Zmittag (m)	Mouse	Muus (f)	opposite (prep)	gägänüber
Lunch break	Mittagspausä (f)	Mouse	Müsli (n)	orange (colour)	orangsch
Lynx	Luchs (m)	Mouth	Muul (n)	Orange	Orangschä (f)
		move out (verb)	uusziä	Orange juice	Orangschäsaft (m)
M		much	vill	Orange juice	O-Saft (m)
		Museum	Museum (n)	order (verb)	pschtelä
Magazine	Heftli (n)	Music	Musig (f)	Oven	Ofä (m)
Magic	Zauberai (f)			over (prep)	über
magic, to do (verb)	zaubärä	N		Overtime	Überschtundä (pl)
Mailbox	Briäfchaschtä (m)			Owner	Psizzer/in (m/f)
Main course	Hauptschpiis (f)	Nail	Nagel (m)		
Make-up	Schminkzüg (n)	Napkin	Serviettä (f)	P	
Manager	Manager/in (m/f) (Mänätscher/in)	National news	Inland-Nachrichtä (pl)		
		Neck	Nakkä (f)	Packet	Päkkli (n)
many	vill	Neighbours	Nachbarä (pl)	Pain	Schmärzä (pl)
Map	Chartä (f)	Nephew	Näffä (m)	Pain Killer	Schmärzmittel (n)
March	März (m)	news	Nachrichtä (pl)	Painful	schmärzhaft
		Newspaper	Zitig (f)	Pan	Pfanä (f)

Panties	Underhosä (f)	Post office	Poscht (f)	Room service	Zimmerservice (m)
Paper towel	Papiertuäch (n)	Postage stamp	Poschtschtämpfel (m)		*(Zimmer-Serwis)*
Parasite	Parasit (m)	Postal money order	Gäldüberwiisig (f)	Rooster	Güggel (m)
Parent's home	Elterähuus (n)	Postcard	Poschtchartä (f)	Rubbish bin	Apfall(chübel) (m)
Park	Park (m)	Postcode	Poschtlaitzaal (f)	Rucksack	Rukksakk (m)
Parking area	Parkplazz (m)	Postman	Pöschtler/in (m/f)		
Part time	tailziit	Potatoes	Herdöpfel (m)	S	
Partner	Partner/in (m/f)	Prawns	Riisecrevettä (f)		
Partner (love)	Läbäs-Partner/in (m/f)		*(Riisägröwettä)*	sad	truurig
Party	Party (f) *(Parti)*	pray (verb)	bätä	Salad	Salat (m)
Party	Fäscht (n)	Prescription	Rezäpt (n)	Salami	Salami (m)
Passenger	Passaschiir (m)	present	jezt	Salary	Loon (m)
Passport	Pass (m)	Present	Gägäwart (f)	Salary	Salär (n)
past	vergangä	Presentation	Präsentazion (f)	Sale (rebate)	Uusverchauff
Past	Vergangähait (f)	press (verb)	drukkä	Salesperson	Verchoiffer/in (m/f)
Pasta	Pasta (f)	Price	Priis (m)	Salmon	Lachs (m)
Pasta	Taigwarä (pl)	Professional	Profi (m)	salty	salzig
Pastry	Gebäkk (n)	Profit	Profit (m)	Sandwich	Sandwich (m)
Path	Wäg (m)	Public telephone	öffentlichs Telefon (n)		*(Sändwitsch)*
Patient	Paziänt/in (m/f)	Punch	Punsch (m)	Satellite	Satellit (m)
pay (verb)	zalä	Purchase order	Pschtellig (f)	Satellite Dish	Satellitäschüsslä (f)
Payment	Zalig (f)	Purchase order	Uuftrag (m)	Saturday	Samschtig
peaceful	fridlich (slang)	Purse	Handtäschli (n)	Sausage	Wurscht (f)
Peak	Gipfel (m)			save (verb)	schparä
Peanut butter	Erdnussbutter (m)	R		Savings account	Schparkonto (n)
Pear	Birä (f)			Scales	Waag (f)
Penis	Penis (m)	Rabbit	Chüngel (m)	Scarf	Schal (m)
Pension fund	Pensionskassä (f)	Rabies	Tollwuät (f)	Scarf	Tuäch (n)
Pension number	Ahavau-Nummerä (f)	Radio	Radio (m)	School	Schuäl (f)
Pepper	Pepperoni (f)	Rain	Räge (m)	Sea	Meer (n)
Perch	Egli (m)	Rappen	Rappä (m)	Seafood	Meeresfrücht (pl)
Perch	Barsch (m)	rare	bluetig	Season	Jaaresziit (f)
Permit	Bewilligung (f)	Raspberry	Himbeeri (n)	second	zwait
Permit	Genemigung (f)	raw	roo	Second (time)	Sekundä (f)
Petrol	Bänzin (n)	Razor blades	Rasiärklingä (f)	Secretary	Sekretär/in (m/f)
Petrol station	Tankschtell (f)	read (verb)	läsä	Section	Apschnitt (m)
Phone call	Aaruäf (m)	Reception	Empfang (m)	Section	Tail (m)
Phone number	Telefonnummerä (f)	Reception	Rezepzion (f)	Security	Sicherhait (f)
Photo	Foti (n)	Receptionist	Resepzionischt/in (m/f)	see (verb)	gsee
Pie	Wäjä (f)	red	rot	sell (verb)	verchauffä
Pig	Sau (f)	Red wine	Rotwii (m) / Rotä (m)	send (verb)	sändä
Pike	Hecht (m)	Registered letter	igschribnä Briäf (m)	send (verb)	schikkä
Pillow	Chüssi (n)	Relatives	Verwandti (pl)	Sender's address	Apsänder/in (m/f)
pink	rosa	Remote control	Fernbediänig (f)	sentimental	sentimental
Plan	Plan (m)	Rental flat	Mietwonig (f)	separate (verb)	sich tränä
Plane ticket	Flugzüg-Tikket (n)	reply (verb)	antwortä	separated	trännt
Plate	Täller (m)	reply (verb)	zruggschriibä	September	Septämber (m)
Platform	Perron (n)	Report	Pricht (m)	Service area	Raschtplazz (m)
play (verb)	geimä	reserve (verb)	reserviärä	Service area	Raschtschtettä (f)
play (verb)	schpilä	Residence permit	Ufenthaltsgenemigung (f)	seven	sibä
play football (verb)	tschutä	Restaurant	Reschtorant (m)	seventeen	sibzä
please	bitte	Restaurant	Baiz (f)	seventh	sibät
Plug	Schtekker (m)	Rhinoceros	Nashorn (n)	seventy	sibäzg
plus	plus	Rice	Riis (m)	sexy	sexy
plus (maths)	und	right	rächts	shake (verb)	schüttlä
Poison	Gift (n)	River	Fluss (m)	Shame, what a	Schad!
poisoned	vergiftet	roasted	gröschtet	Shampoo	Schampoo (n)
Polyester	Polyester (m)	Roe	Ree (n)	Sheet	Bettuäch (n)
	(Polijeschter)	Roll	Brötli (n)	Shirt	Hämp (n)
Pork	Schwinigs (n)	Roll	Pürli (n)	Shoes	Schuä (pl)
Pork	Schwaineflaisch (n)	Roof	Tach (n)	Shop	Ladä (m)
Post	Poscht (f)	Room	Zimmer (n)	shop (verb)	iichauffä

shopping (go)	lädälä	Speed limit	Gschwindigkaits-	tasteless	fad
Shopping bag	Iichaufs-Täschä (f)		[begränzig (f)	tasteless	gschmakklos
Shopping centre	Ichaufszentrum (n)	spend (verb)	uusgä	Taxes	Schtürä (pl)
short	churz	spicy	scharf	Tea	Tee (m)
short sleeves	churzärmlig	Spider	Schpinä (f)	Teaspoon	Teelöffeli (n)
Shorts	Shorts (pl)	Spinach	Schpinat (m)	Technician	Techniker/in (m/f)
short-sighted	churzsichtig	Spirit	Schnaps (m)	Teenager	Teeni (m) *(Tiini)*
Shoulder	Schulterä (f)	Spoon	Löffel (m)	telephone (verb)	aalütä
Shower	Duschi (f)	Sports	Schport (m)	Telephone bill	Telefonrächnig (f)
Shower cream	Duschmittel (n)	Spring	Früälig (m)	Telephone book	Telefonbüäch (n)
Shower curtain	Duschvorhang (m)	Stairs	Schtägä (f)	Telephone card	Telefonchartä (f)
Shrimp	Crevettä (f) *(Gröwettä)*	Stamp	Markä (f)	Television	Fernse (n)
shy	schüch	stare (verb)	schtarrä	Television licence	Fernsebewilligung (f)
Siblings	Gschwüschterti (pl)	Starter	Vorschpiis (f)	Temperature	Temperatur (f)
sick	chrank	State	Schtaat (m)	ten	zä
Signature	Unterschrift (f)	Steak	Steak (n) *(Steik)*	Tenant	Mieter/in (m/f)
Silk	Sidä (f)	Stockings	Schtrümpf (pl)	Tennis Shoes	Tennisschuä (pl)
silver (colour)	silber	Stomach	Magä (m)	tenth	zät
single	ledig	Stomachache	Buuchwee (n)	Terrace	Terrassä (f)
single	single	Store	Ladä (m)	Text message	SMS (n) *(Äsämäs)*
Sister	Schwö(schter) (f)	Storm	Schturm (m)	thank you	danke
Sister-in-law	Schwögerin (f)	Stove	Härd (m)	thank you	merci (märsi)
six	sächs	straight on	graduus	thousand	tuusig
sixteen	sächzä	Strawberry	Erdbeeri (n)	Theatre	Theater (n)
sixth	sächst	Street	Schtrass (f)	there	deet
sixty	sächzg	stressed	gschtresst	Thief	Diäb (m)
Skin	Huut (f)	Studio	Schtudio (n)	thing	Sach (f)
Skirt	Rokk (m)	stupid	blööd	thing	Ding (n)
Skirt	Jupe (m) *(Schüpp)*	stupid	doof	third	dritt
Slug	Schnägg (m)	Subject	Thema (n)	thirsty	Durscht (m)
sleepy	müäd	suck (verb)	sugä	thirteen	drizä
sleepy	schlapp	Sugar	Zukker (m)	thirty	drissg
sleepy	schlöfrig	Suit (for man)	Aazug (m)	three	drü
Slippers	Finkä (pl)	Suit (for woman)	Koschtüm (n)	Throat	Hals (m)
small	chlii	Summer	Summer (m)	through (prep)	dur(ch)
smell	schmökkä	Sun	Sunä (f)	Thunder	Dunner (m)
smile	lächlä	Sunday	Sunntig	Thunderstorm	Gwitter (n)
Smoking area	Rauchereggä (m)	sunny	sunig	Thursday	Dunnschtig
Snack (afternoon)	Zvieri (m)	Sunshade	Sunätach (n)	Tie	Grawattä (f)
Snack (morning)	Znüni (m)	super	hammer (slang)	Tiger	Tiger (m)
Snake	Schlangä (f)	super	mega (slang)	to (prep)	zu
Snow	Schnee (m)	Supermarket	Supermärt (m)	Toast	Tooscht (m)
Soap	Soiffä (f)	surprised	überrascht	Today	hüt
Society	Gsellschaft (f)	sweet	süäss	Toe	Zäjä (m)
Socks	Sokkä (pl)	sweetie	Schnugi	Toenail	Zäjänagel (m)
Soft drink	Blöterliwasser (n)	swim (verb)	schwümä	Toilet	Toilettä (f) *(Tualettä)*
some	äs paar	Swimming pool	Schwümmbad (n)	Toilet	WC (n) *(Weze)*
some	ainigi	Swiss accordion	Handörgeli (n)	Toiletry bag	Necessaire (n)
somebody	öpper	Swiss Francs	Schwiizer Frankä (m)		*(Nessessär)*
somehow	irgendwiä	Swiss wrestling	schwingä	Toilet paper	WC-Papier (n)
something	öppis	Synagogue	Synagogä (f)		*(Weze-Papier)*
sometimes	mängisch			Toiletries	Badzimmersachä (pl)
somewhere	noimät	**T**		Tomato	Tomatä (f)
Son	Soon (m)			Tomorrow	morn
Son-in-law	Schwigersoon (m)	Table	Tisch (m)	Tongue	Zungä (f)
soon	bald	Table cloth	Tischtüäch (n)	Tooth	Zaa (m)
sorry	sorry	Table mats	Tischmattä (f)	Toothbrush	Zaabürschteli (n)
so-so	so so (la la)	Take away	Take away (m)	Toothpaste	Zaapaschtä (f)
sour	suur		*(Teik Awei)*	Top	Obertail (n)
Space	Ruum (m)	Talk show	Talk Show (f)	Top floor	oberschti Schtokk (m)
speak (verb)	redä		*(Tok Schou)*	touch (verb)	berüärä
Speed camera	Radar (m)	Tangerine	Mandarinli (n)	touch (verb)	aalangä

Dictionary

Tourist	Turischt/in (m/f)	Valley	Taal (n)	White wine	Wiissä (m)
Tourist	Turi (m) (slang)	Veal	Chalbflaisch (n)	Who?	Wär?
Towel	Tüächli (n)	vegan	vegan(isch)	Whole grain bread	Vollkornbrot (n)
Town	Schtadt (f)	Vegetables	Gmüäs (n)	Why?	Warum?
Track	Glais (n)	vegetarian	vegetarisch	wide	wiit
Traffic light	Amplä (f)	vigorous	energisch	Widow	Witwe (f)
Train	Zug (m)	Village	Dörfli (n)	widowed	verwitwet
Train station	Baanhof (m)	Vinegar	Essig (m)	Widower	Witwer (m)
Train ticket	Zugbilet (n)	violet	violett	Wife	Frau (f)
Trainee	Praktikant/in (m/f)	Virus	Wirus (m)	wiggle (verb)	gwagglä
transfer (verb)	überwiisä	Visa	Wisum (n)	Wild boar	Wildsau (f)
Trash	Apfallchorb (m)			Wind	Wind (m)
Travellers' cheque	Traveller cheques (pl)	W		Wind surfing	Wind sörfä
	(Träwälär Schegg)			Window	Fänschter (n)
Tree	Baum (m)	Waist	Talliä (f)	Wine	Wii (m)
Trousers	Hosä (f)	Wake up call	Wekkaaruäf (m)	wink (verb)	zwinkerä
Trout	Forälä (f)	Ward	Schtazion(f)	Winter	Winter (m)
T-Shirt	T-Shirt (n)	Ward	Aptailig (f) (f)	with (prep)	mit
T-Shirt	Liibli (n)	Wardrobe	Gardärobä (f)	withdraw (verb)	abhebä
Tuesday	Ziischtig	Warehouse	Lagerhallä (f)	without	ooni
Tumble drier	Tumbler (m)(Tömbler)	Warehouse	Warähuus (n)	Wolf	Wolf (m)
Tuna	Ton (m)	warm	warm	Wool	Wulä (f)
Turkey	Truthaan (m)	Washbasin	Brüneli (n)	Worker	Arbaiter/in (m/f)
Turtle	Schildchrot (f)	Washbasin	Lavabo (n)	World	Wält (f)
twelve	zwölf	wash (verb)	wäschä	Worm	Wurm (m)
twenty	zwänzg	Washing machine	Wöschmaschine (f)	worried	besorgt
Twins	Zwilling (pl)	Wasp	Wäschpi (n)		
two	zwai	watch (verb)	luägä		
two hundred	zwaihundert	Water with gas	Wasser mit Cholesüüri		
two thousand	zwaituusig	Water without gas	Wasser ooni	Y	
Two-room apt.	Zwaizimmerwonig(f)		Cholesüüri		
		Watermelon	Wassermelonä (f)	yawn (verb)	gäänä
U		Weather	Wätter (n)	Year	Jaar (n)
		Weather report	Wätterpricht (m)	yellow	gääl
Uncle	Unggle (m)	Wedding	Hochziit (f)	yes	ja
under (prep)	under	Wedding eve's party	Polteraabig (m)	Yesterday	geschter
Underwear	Underwösch (f)	Wednesday	Mittwuch	yodel (verb)	jodlä
Uniform	Uniform (f)	Week	Wuchä (f)	Yoghurt	Joghurt (n) (Jogurt)
Unlucky number	Ungl ükkszaal (f)	Weekend	Wuchänänd (n)	young man	Purscht (m)
until (prep)	bis	Welcome	Willkomä	young man	jungä Maa (m)
Up	ufä	What ?	Was ?	young woman	jungi Frau (f)
Urinal	Pissoir (n) (Pissuar)	When?	Wänn?	young woman	Frölain (n)
Utility room	Apschtellruum (m)	Where to?	Wohi?		
		Where?	Wo?	Z	
V		whisper (verb)	flüschterä		
		white	wiiss	Zebra	Zebra (n)
vacant	frei	White bread	Wiissbrot (n)	zero	null
Vacations	Feriä (pl)	White fish	Felchä (f)	Zoo	Zoo (m)
Vagina	Vagina (f)	White wine	Wiisswii (m)		

This way to the Swiss German to English Dictionary

Swiss German
to
English

A

a	at (prep)
a(m)	on (vert.surface) (prep)
Aabigchlaid (n)	Evening dress
aalangä	touch (verb)
Aalass (m)	Event
aalütä	telephone (verb)
Aaruäf (m)	Phone call
aaziiä	dress (verb)
aazogä	dressed
Aazug (m)	Suit
abä	down
abfaarä	leave (verb)
abhebä	withdraw (verb)
Aabig (m)	Evening
Aabigdämmerig (f)	Dusk
Abrais (f)	Departure
Abwäschmaschine(f)	Dishwasher
acht	eight
äis	one
acht	eighth
Achtung	careful
achzä	eighteen
achtzg	eighty
Addrässbuäch (n)	Address book
adieu *(adjö)*	Bye
Adler (m)	Eagle
Adrässä (f)	Address
Aff (m)	Monkey
Agschtellte (m)	Employee
Agschtellti (f)	Employee
Ahavau-Nummerä(f)	Pension number
Ai (n)	Egg
Aidächsli (n)	Lizard
(ain)-tuusig	one thousand
ainigi	some
ainsam	lonely
Aizimmerwonig (f)	One-room apt.
Akunft (f)	Arrival
Alergii (f)	Allergy
alergisch gägä	allergic to
Alphorn (m)	Alpenhorn
altä Maa	old man
Altbau (m)	old building
alti Frau	old woman

Amaisä (f)	Ant
Ambulanz (f)	Ambulance
Amplä (f)	Traffic light
anglä	fish (verb)
ängschtlich	afraid
ängschtlich	anxious
Ankä (m)	Butter
Änkel (m)	Grandson
Änkelin (f)	Granddaughter
antwortä	reply (verb)
Aperitif (m)	Appetizer
Apero (m)	Appetizer
Apfallchorb (m)	Trash
Apfallchübel (m)	Rubbish bin
Apsänder/in (m/f)	Sender's address
Apschidsfäscht (n)	Farewell party
Apschnitt (m)	Section
Apschtellruum (m)	Utility room
Apszäss (m)	Abscess
Aptailig (f)	Ward
Aptailig (f)	Department
April (m)	April
Arbaiter/in	Worker
Arbetgeber/in (m/f)	Employer
Arbetskolleg/in (m/f)	Colleague
Arbetsmappä (f)	Briefcase
Arm (m)	Arm
Armbruscht (schüssä)	Crossbow(shooting)
Aromat (n)	Condiment
Artikel (m)	Article
Arzt (m)	Doctor
Ärztin (f)	Doctor
äs paar	some
Aschlagbrätt (n)	Bulletin board
Aschtma (n)	Asthma
Aschpirin (n)	Aspirin
aschtekkänd	contagious
Asischtänt/in (m/f)	Assistant
Ässzimmer (n)	Dining room
Attachment (n)	Attachment
(Attätschmänt)	
Attikawonig (f)	Attic flat
Aug (n)	Eye
Augebrauä (f)	Eyebrow
Auguscht (m)	August
Auto (n)	Car
Autobaan (f)	Highway

B

B&B (n)	B&B
Baanhof (m)	Train station
Badzimmer (n)	Bathroom
Badwannä (f)	Bath tub
Badzimmersachä (pl)	Toiletries
Baggä (m)	Cheek
Bai (n)	Leg
Baiz (f)	Restaurant
bald	soon
Balkon (m)	Balcony
Bananä (f)	Banana
Bank (f)	Bank

Bankkonto (n)	Bank account
Banknotä (f)	Banknotes
Bänzin (n)	Petrol
Bar (f)	Bar
Bär (m)	Bear
Bärg (m)	Mountain
Bargäld (n)	Cash
Barsch (m)	Perch
bätä	pray (verb)
Baum (m)	Tree
Baumwule (f)	Cotton
bedekkt	cloudy
Beha (m)	Bra
beige (bäsch)	beige
Bekk (m)	Bakery
Bekkerei (f)	Bakery
Berater/in (m/f)	Consultant
Berliner (m)	Jam doughnut
berüämt / bekannt	famous
berüärä	touch (verb)
Beschprächig (f)	Meeting
besorgt	worried
Bett (n)	Bed
Bettaazug (m)	Bed cover
Bettdekki (f)	Duvet
Bettuäch (n)	Sheet
Bewärbig (f)	Job application
Bewärbigsgschpräch(n)	Job interview
Bewilligung (f)	Permit
bi	at (prep)
bi	by (prep)
Biändli (n)	Bee
Biär (n)	Beer
Bibliothek (f)	Library
biigä (slang)	eat (verb)
Biinä (f)	Bee
Bilet (n)	Driver's licence
Birä (f)	Pear
bis	by (prep)
bis	until (prep)
bitte	please
bitter	bitter
blau	blue
blau (slang)	drunk
blasä	blow (verb)
Blinddarmenzündig(f)	Appendicitis
blinzlä	blink (verb)
Blizz (m)	Lightning
blööd	stupid
Blöterliwasser (n)	Soft drink
Bluämächöl (m)	Cauliflower
Bluät (n)	Blood
Bluätdrukk (m)	Blood pressure
Bluätzukker (m)	Blood sugar
bluetig	rare
Blusä (f)	Blouse
Bodä (m)	Floor
Bölä (pl)	Onion
Bonus (m)	Bonus
Boonä (f)	Beans
bös	angry
Bratpfanä (f)	Frying pan

Briäf (m)	Letter	Chnobli (m)	Garlic	Digestive (m)	Digestive
Briäfchaschtä (m)	Mailbox	Chnochäbruch (m)	Broken bone	*(Dischestiv)*	
Broggoli (m)	Broccoli	Chnöchel (m)	Ankle	Ding (n)	Thing
Brot (m)	Bread	Chnopf (m)	Button	Diräktor/in (m/f)	Director
Brötli (n)	Roll	Chnü (n)	Knee	Disco (f)	Discotheque
Brüäder (m)	Brother	Chopf (m)	Head	doof	stupid
brüälä	cry (verb)	Chopfsalat (m)	Lettuce	Doolä (f)	Jackdaw
Brugg (f)	Bridge	Chopfwee (n)	Headache	Doppelbett (n)	Double bed
Brunch (m)	Brunch	Choschtä (pl)	Costs	Dörfli (n)	Village
Brüneli (n)	Washbasin	Chragä (m)	Collar	drissg	thirty
Bruscht (f)	Chest	Chrampf (m)	Cramp	dritt	third
Bruschtwarzä (f)	Nipple	chrank	sick	drizä	thirteen
bruun	brown	Chrankäschwöschter (f)	Nurse	drü	three
Buäb (m)	Boy	Chrankäwagä (m)	Ambulance	drukkä	press (verb)
Büäbli (n)	Baby boy	Chriäsi (n)	Cherry	dunkel	dark
Buäch (n)	Book	Chrüüzig (f)	Crossing	dunkels Brot (n)	brown bread
Büächergschtell (n)	Book shelves	Chuä (f)	Cow	Dunner (m)	Thunder
Büächerladä (m)	Bookshop	Chüälschrank (m)	Fridge	Dunnschtig	Thursday
Büächhandlig (f)	Bookshop	Chuchi (f)	Kitchen	dur(ch)	through (prep)
Buchnabel (m)	Bellybutton	Chuchiablagä (pl)	Kitchen shelves	Durchfall (m)	Diarrhoea
Bügälisä (n)	Iron	Chuächä (m)	Cake	Durscht (m)	Thirsty
Büro (n)	Office	chüel	cool (temperat.)	Duschi (f)	Shower
Bürschtä (f)	Brush	Chund/in (m/f)	Customer	Duschmittel (n)	Shower cream
Bus (m)	Bus	Chüngel (m)	Rabbit	Duschvorhang (m)	Shower curtain
Busä (m)	Breast	churz	short		
Busbilet (n)	Bus ticket	churzärmlig	short sleeves	E	
Busbaanhof (m)	Bus station	churzsichtig	short-sighted		
Büsi (n)	Cat	Chüssi (n)	Pillow	EC-Chartä (f)	Debit card
Bushalteschtell (f)	Bus stop	ciao *(tschau)*	Bye (informal)	*(Eze-Chartä)*	
Butter (m)	Butter	City (f) *(Sitti)*	City	Eggä (m)	Corner
Buuch (m)	Abdomen	Coggi (n)	Coke	Egli (m)	Perch
Buuchwee (n)	Stomachache	Consierge (m)	Concierge	Ehe (f)	Marriage
		(Gonsiersch)		Elefant (m)	Elephant
C		cool	cool (kuul)	Elektrogschäft (n)	Electrical shop
		Cousine (f) *(Gusinä)*	Cousin	elf	eleven
Cappuccino (m)	Cappuccino	Cousin (m) *(Gusän)*	Cousin	Eläbogä (m)	Elbow
(Gaputschino)		Couvert (n) *(Kuwäär)*	Envelope	Elterähuus (n)	Parent's home
Cash *(Käsch)*	Cash	Crème (f) *(Gräm)*	Cream	Empfang (m)	Reception
Chäfer (m)	Beetle	Crevettä (f) *(Gröwettä)*	Shrimp	energisch	vigorous
Chalbflaisch (n)	Veal			entlang	along (prep)
Chäller (m)	Cellar	D		entschuldigung	Excuse me
chalt	cold			enttüscht	disappointed
Chalti Getränk (pl)	cold drinks	da	here	Enzündig (f)	Infection
Chalti Schoggi (f)	cold chocolate	Dämmerig (f)	Dawn	Erdbeeri (n)	Strawberry
Chämi (n)	Chimney	Dämmerig (f)	Dusk	Erdnussbutter (m)	Peanut butter
Chappä (f)	Cap	dankbar	grateful	erscht	first
Chartä (f)	Map	danke	thank you	erschtä Schtokk	first floor
Chäs (m)	Cheese	Darleä (n)	Loan	Erschti Hilf (f)	First Aid
Chaschtä (m)	Closet	deet	there	erschtunt	amazed
chauffä	buy (verb)	deitä	date (verb)	Erwachsenä/i (m/f)	Adult
Chazz (f)	Cat	Dekadä (f)	Decade	Eschtrich (m)	Attic
Chef/in (m/f) *(Schef/in)*	Boss	Delikatessladä (m)	Deli(katessen)	Esel (m)	Donkey
Cheminée(n) *(Schminee)*	Fireplace	Deo (m)	Deodorant	Espresso (m)	Expresso
Chilä (f)	Church	Depot (n) *(Depo)*	Deposit (money)	Essig (m)	Vinegar
Chinderzimmer (n)	Children's room	depressiv	depressed	Event (m) *(iwent)*	Event
Chischtä (f)	Box	Desktop (m)	Desktop	exgüsi	Excuse me
Chlaid (n)	Dress (noun)	Dessert (m)	Dessert		
Chlaider (pl)	Clothing	Dezämber (m)	December	F	
Chlaiderbügel (m)	Hanger	Diäb (m)	Thief		
Chlaidervorschrift (f)	Dress code	Diabetis (f)	Diabetes	Faanä (f)	Flag
chlii	small	diabetisch	diabetic	Faaruuswis (m)	Driver's licence
Chnoblauch (m)	Garlic	Diät (f)	Diet	fad	tasteless

Fäld (n)	Field	**G**		grau	grey
Faltä	fold (verb)			grüän	green
Familiäschluuch (m)	Family get-together	gääl	yellow	Grawattä (f)	Tie
		gäänä	yawn (verb)	grüffä	grap (verb)
Familiäschtand (m)	Marital status	Gablä (f)	Fork	griliert	grilled
Familiäzämäkunft (f)	Family get-together	gaga	crazy	Grill (m)	Grill
		gägä	against (prep)	Grillfäscht (n)	Barbecue
Fänschter (n)	Window	gägä	into (prep)	Grippe (f)	Flu
fantastisch	fantastic	Gägägift (n)	Antidote	gröschtet	roasted
Fäscht (n)	Party	gägänüber	across from (prep)	Groselterä (pl)	Grandparents
Fasnacht (f)	Carnival	gägänüber	opposite (prep)	Grosmuetter (f)	Grandmother
Februar (m)	February	Gägäwart (f)	Present	Grosunggle (m)	Great uncle
Felchä (f)	White fish	Gaiss (f)	Goat	gross	big
Feriä (pl)	Vacations	Gäld (n)	Money	gross	large
Fernbediänig (f)	Remote control	Gäld inweschtierä	invest money	Gros-chind (n)	Grandchild
Fernse (n)	Television	Gäld verdiänä	earn money	Grostantä (f)	Great aunt
Fernsebewilligung (f)	Television licence	Gäldautomat (m)	Cash machine	Grosvatter (m)	Grandfather
feschthebä	grap (verb)	Gäldüberwiisig (f)	Postal money order	Grüezi	Hello
Fiäber (n)	Fever	gämblä	to gamble	Gschäft (n)	Business
Finger (m)	Finger	Gämsi (f)	Chamois	gschidä	divorced
Fingernagel (m)	Fingernail	Gang (m)	Hallway	Gschirr (n)	Dishes
Finkä (pl)	Slippers	Garage (f) (Garasch)	Garage	Gschmakk (m)	Flavour
Fisch (m)	Fish	Gardärobä (f)	Wardrobe	gschmakklos	tasteless
fischä	fish (verb)	Gartä (m)	Garden	gschtresst	stressed
Fitness	Fitness	Gebäkk (n)	Pastry	Gschwindigkaits-	Speed limit
Fitnessruum (m)	Gym	Geboide (n)	Building	[begränzig (f)	
Flaisch (n)	Meat	Gebür (f)	Fee	Gschwüschterti (pl)	Siblings
Flügä (f)	Fly	Geburtstags-party (f)	Birthday party	gsee	see
Flugzüg (n)	Aeroplane	gedigä (slang)	comfortable	Gsellschaft (f)	Society
Flugzüg-Tikket (n)	Flight ticket	geimä	to play	Gsicht (n)	Face
flüschterä	whisper (verb)	Genemigung (f)	Permit	guet	good
Fluss (m)	River	Geografii (f)	Geography	Güggel (m)	Rooster
Flusspferd (n)	Hippopotamus	Gepäkk (n)	Luggage	gumpä	jump (verb)
föif	five	geschter	Yesterday	Gurt (m)	Belt
Föön (m)	Foehn	Ghaimnummerä (f)	Code (secret)	Gürtel (m)	Belt
Forälä (f)	Trout	Ghirnerschütterig (f)	Concussion	gwagglä	wiggle (verb)
Formular (n)	Form	ghörä	hear (verb)	Gwitter (n)	Thunderstorm
forwardä	forward (verb)	Gift (n)	Poison	Gwürz (pl)	Condiment
Foti (n)	Photo	giggerig	horny		
frei	vacant	Gipfel (m)	Peak	**H**	
Frau (f)	Wife	Gipfeli (n)	Croissant		
fridlich (slang)	peaceful	git	equals	Haanä (m)	Faucet/ tap
Friitig	Friday	gkocht	boiled	Haar (pl)	Hair
frittiert	deep fried	Glacé (n) (Glasse)	Ice cream	Hagel (m)	Hail
Frölain (n)	young woman	Glais (n)	Track	haglä	hail (verb)
froo	joyful	glangwiilet	bored	Hailmittel (n)	Medicine
fröölich	cheerful	Glas (n)	Glass	haimelig	cosy
früä	early	Glüäwii (m)	hot wine	haiss	hot
Früälig (m)	Spring	glükklich	happy	haissi Milch (f)	hot milk
Frucht (f)	Fruit	Glükkszaal (f)	lucky number	haissi Schoggi (f)	hot chocolate
Fründ/in (m/f)	Friend	Gmüäs (n)	Vegetables	halal	halal
früsch	fresh	gmüätlich	cosy	halb durä	medium (meat)
Fuäss (m)	Foot	gold	gold (colour)	Halbpension (f)	Half board
Fuchs (m)	Fox	Gomfi (f)	Jam	Hals (m)	Throat
Füdli (n)	Bottom	görpsä	burp (verb)	hammer (slang)	super
füecht	humid	görpslä (Babys)	burp (verb)	Hämp (n)	Shirt
füft	fifth	gradi Zaalä	even numbers	Hand (f)	Hand
füfzä	fifteen	graduus	straight on	Handcreme (f)	Hand cream
füfzg	fifty	Gränzä (f)	Border	(Handgräm)	
für	for (prep)	Gränzä (f)	Frontier	Handörgeli (n)	Swiss accordion
Füür (n)	Fire	Grapefruitsaft (m)	Grapefruit juice	Händtröchner (m)	Hand dryer
		(Gräpfrüsaft)		Händi(n)	Mobile phone

Häntschä (pl)	Gloves	in	in (prep)	Konzärt (n)	Concert
Härd (m)	Stove	in	into (prep)	kopierä	copy (verb)
Härpscht (m)	Autumn	Inland-Nachrichtä(pl)	National news	Körperlozioon (f)	Body lotion
Härz (n)	Heart	Insekt (n)	Insect	koscher	kosher
härzig	lovely	Inslä (f)	Island	Koschtüm (n)	Suit (for woman)
hässig	furious	Intensivschtazion (f)	Intensive care	Krabä (f)	Crab
Hauptschpiis (f)	Main course	internazionalä	long distance call	Kreditchartä (f)	Credit card
hebä	hold (verb)	[Aaruäf (m)		Krokodil (n)	Crocodile
Hecht (m)	Pike	Inweschtierig (f)	Investment	Kultur (f)	Culture
Heftli (n)	Magazine	Inweschtizion (f)	Investment	Kunscht (f)	Art
hell	light	irgendöppis	anything	Kurs (m)	Course
Herdöpfel (m)	Potatoes	irgendwiä	somehow	küssä	kiss (verb)
Herusgeber/in (m/f)	Editor	irr	crazy	kuul (slang)	Cool
hetero(sexuell)	heterosexual	isch glich	equals		
Hilfe (f)	help			**L**	
Himbeeri (n)	Raspberry	**J**			
hinder	behind (prep)			Läbäs-Partner/in (m/f)	Partner (love)
Hinderlegig (f)	Deposit (money)	ja	yes	Läbere (f)	Liver
Hirsch (m)	Deer	Jaar (n)	Year	Läbesmittel (pl)	Groceries
Hizz (f)	Heat	Jaaresziit (f)	Season	Labor (n)	Laboratory
Hochziit (f)	Wedding	Jaarhundert (n)	Century	lachä	laugh (verb)
Hoi	Hi (informal)	Jaartuusig (n)	Millennium	lächlä	smile
Hoi zäme	Hi (to several)	Jagge (f)	Jacket	Lachs (m)	Salmon
Hoischnuppä (m)	Hay fever	Januar (m)	January	Ladä (m)	Shop
homo(sexuell)	homosexual	Jeans (pl) (Tschins)	Jeans	Ladä (m)	Store
Honig (m)	Honey	jezt	present	lädälä	shopping (go)
Hosä (f)	Trousers	jezt	now	Läder (n)	Leather
Huän (n)	Chicken	Job (m) (Tschop)	Occupation	Lagerhallä (f)	Warehouse
Huänerhuut (f)	Goose bumps	Jobbeschribig (f)	Job description	Laischtigsbewärtig (f)	Appraisal
huäschtä	cough (verb)	jodlä	yodel (verb)	Lamm (n)	Lamb
Huät (m)	Hat	Joghurt (n) (Jogurt)	Yoghurt	Land (n)	Country
Hüft (f)	Hip	Juli (m)	July	landä	land (verb)
Hügel (m)	Hill	jungä Maa (m)	young man	lang	long
Hülsäfrücht (pl)	Legumes	jungi Frau (f)	young woman	langärmlig	long sleeves
Hummer (m)	Lobster	Juni (m)	June	Laptop (m) (Läptop)	Laptop
Humoor (m)	Humour	Jupe (m) (Schüpp)	Skirt	läsä	read (verb)
Hund (m)	Dog			Latte Macchiato (f)	Latte Macchiato
hundert	hundred	**K**		(Maggiato)	
hunderttuusig	hundred thousand			Lavabo (n)	Washbasin
Hunger (m)	hungry	Kabelfernse (n)	Cable TV	Lawinä (f)	Avalanche
Husiweiigs-party (f)	Housewarming	Kafi (crème) (m)	Coffee with cream	ledig	single
hüt	Today	Kafi (n)	Coffee bar / cafe	Leerling (m)	Apprentice
hüüla	cry (verb)	Kafichränzli (n)	Coffee party	lesbisch	lesbian
Huusgloggä (f)	Doorbell	Kafiklatsch (m)	Coffee party	liäbä	love (verb)
Huusnummerä (f)	House number	Kafipausä (f)	Coffee break	Lift (m)	Lift
Huut (f)	Skin	Kakerlakä (f)	Cockroach	Liibli (n)	T-Shirt
		Kanal (m)	Channel	Liinä (f)	Linen
I		känslä	cancel (verb)	lila	Lilac
		Kantinä (f)	Canteen	Limone (f)	Lime
Ichaufszentrum (n)	Shopping centre	Kanton (m)	County	linggs	left
ifersüchtig	jealous	Kassierer/in (m/f)	Cashier	Linsä (pl)	Lentils
igschribnä Briäf (m)	Registered letter	Katedraale (f)	Cathedral	Löffel (m)	Spoon
igschribni Poscht (f)	Registered mail	Kino (n)	Cinema	Loi (n)	Lion
iichauffä	shop (verb)	Klatsch (m)	Gossip	lokale Aaruäf (m)	Local call
Iichaufs-Täschä (f)	Shopping bag	klatschä	gossip (verb)	lokali Nachrichtä (pl)	Local news
Iigang (m)	Entrance	Klima (n)	Climate	lokali Noiigkaitä (pl)	Local news
Iigangshallä (f)	Entry way	Klinik (f)	Clinic	Loon (m)	Salary
Iikomä (n)	Income	Kod (m)	Code	losä	listen (verb)
iiloggä	log in (verb)	Komission (f)	Commission	löschä	cancel (verb)
iiraisä	immigrate (verb)	Kondom (n)	Condom	luägä	look (verb)
Iis-tee (m)	Iced tea	Konfäränz (f)	Conference	luägä	watch (verb)
iitschäggä	check in (verb)	Kontinänt (m)	Continent	Luchs (m)	Lynx

Luftposcht (f) — Airmail
Luftschuzzchäller (m) — Bunker
Lungebröötli(n)(slang) — Cigarette
luschtig — funny
lutschä — lick (verb)

M

Maa (m) — Husband
Määl (n) — Flour
Maalzitä (pl) — Meals
Magä (m) — Stomach
Mai (m) — May
Mainig (f) — Opinion
Mais (m) — Corn
Mais-cholbä (m) — Corn on the cob
Mait(ä)li (n) — Girl
Maitli (n) — Baby girl
mälchä — milk (verb)
Manager/in (m/f) *(Mänätscher/in)* — Manager
Mandarinli (n) — Tangerine
mängisch — sometimes
Mantel (m) — Coat
Mäntig — Monday
Marder (m) — Marten
Margerinä (f) — Margarine
mariniert — marinated
Markä (f) — Brand
Markä (f) — Stamp
März (m) — March
Märzetüpfli (pl) — Freckles
Massage (f) *(Masaasch)* — Massage
Mässer (n) — Knife
mee — more
Meer (n) — Sea
Meeresfrücht (pl) — Seafood
Meersoili (n) — Guinea pig
mega (slang) — super
Mensa (f) — Canteen
merci *(märsi)* — thank you
Mezzg (f) — Butcher's shop
Mieter/in (m/f) — Tenant
Mietwonig (f) — Rental flat
Mikrowälä (f) — Microwave
Milch (f) — Milk
Milchkafi (m) — Coffee with milk
mild — mild
Milliard (f) — billion
Million (f) — million
Mineralwasser (n) — Mineral water
minus — minus
Minutä (f) — Minute
mit — by (transport)(prep)
mit — with (prep)
Mittag (m) — Noon/ midday
Mittagspausä (f) — Lunch break
mittleri Grössi — medium (size)
Mittwuch — Wednesday
Modä (f) — Fashion
Moisebussard (m) — Buzzard

Momänt (m) — moment
Monät (m) — Month
Mönggi (n) (slang) — Idiot
Morgä (m) — Morning
Morgädämmerig (f) — Dawn
morn — Tomorrow
Moschee (f) — Mosque
mozzä (slang) — complain (verb)
müäd — sleepy
Muetter (f) — Mother
Muggä (f) — Mosquito
Mumeltiär (n) — Marmot
Münz (n) — Change (money)
Münzä (f) — Coin
Museum (n) — Museum
Musig (f) — Music
Müsli (n) — Mouse
Muul (n) — Mouth
Muus (f) — Mouse

N

näbäd — beside (prep)
näbäd — next to (prep)
Näbel (m) — Fog
nach — according to (prep)
nach — after (prep)
Nachbarä (pl) — Neighbours
Nachrichtä (pl) — The news
Nacht (f) — Night
Näffä (m) — Nephew
Nagel (m) — Nail
nai — no
Nakkä (f) — Neck
Namittag (m) — Afternoon
Nasä (f) — Nose
Nashorn (n) — Rhinoceros
Natel (n) — Mobile phone
Necessaire (n) *(Nessessär)* — Toiletry bag
Nichtä (f) — Niece
niidisch — envious
Nilpferd (n) — Hippopotamus
Noibau (m) — Building (new)
noimät — somewhere
Notfall (m) — Emergency
Notufnaam (f) — Emergency room
Novämber (m) — November
null — zero
nün — nine
nünt — ninth
nünzä — nineteen
nünzg — ninety
nüt — nothing
Nylon (n) *(Nailon)* — Nylon

O

Oberschinä (f) — Eggplant
oberschti Schtokk (m) — Top floor
Obertail (n) — Top
Ofä (m) — Oven

öffentlichs Telefon (n) — Public telephone
Oktober (m) — October
Olivenöl (n) — Olive oil
ooni — without
Oor (n) — Ear
Operä (f) — Opera
Operazion (f) — Operation
Öpfel (m) — Apple
Öpfelsaft (m) — Apple juice
öpper — somebody
öppis — something
orangsch — orange (colour)
Orangschäsaft (m) — Orange juice
Orangschä (f) — Orange
Orangschägomfi (f) — Marmalade
O-Saft (m) — Orange juice
Ozean (m) — Ocean

P

Päch (n) — Bad luck
Päkkli (n) — Packet
Papiertuäch (n) — Paper towel
Parasit (m) — Parasite
Pariserbrot (n) — Baguette
Park (m) — Park
Parkplazz (m) — Parking area
Partär (n) — Ground floor
Partner/in (m/f) — Partner
Party (f) *(Parti)* — Party
Pass (m) — Passport
Passaschiir (m) — Passenger
Pasta (f) — Pasta
Pausä (f) — Break
Paziänt/in (m/f) — Patient
Penis (m) — Penis
Pensionskassä (f) — Pension fund
Pepperoni (f) — Pepper
Perron (n) — Platform
Pfanä (f) — Pan
Pflägfachfrau (f) — Nurse
Pflägfachmaa (m) — Nurse
Pfläschterli (n) — Band-aid
Pissoir (n) *(Pissuar)* — Urinal
Plan (m) — Plan
plus — plus
Polteraabig (m) — Wedding eve's party
Polteraabig (m) — Hen night
Polyester (m) *(Polijeschter)* — Polyester
Poscht (f) — Post
Poscht (f) — Post office
poschtä — buy (verb)
Poschtchartä (f) — Postcard
Poschtlaitzaal (f) — Postcode
Pöschtler/in (m/f) — Postman
Poschtschtämpfel (m) — Postage stamp
Poulet (n) *(Pule)* — Chicken
Praktikant/in (m/f) — Trainee
Präsentazion (f) — Presentation
Praxis (f) — Doctor's surgery
Pricht (m) — Report

Priis (m)	Fee	Rukksakk (m)	Rucksack	schpilä	to gamble
Priis (m)	Price	Ruum (m)	Space	schpilä	to play
Profi (m)	Professional			Schpinä (f)	Spider
Profit (m)	Profit	S		Schpinat (m)	Spinach
Promi (m)	Celebrity			Schpital (n)	Hospital
Proscht	Cheers	Sach (f)	Thing	schpizz	horny
Pröschtli	Cheers	sächs	six	Schport (m)	Sports
prötlet	fried	sächst	sixth	Schprüzzä (f)	Injection
Protokoll (n)	Minutes	sächzä	sixteen	Schtaat (m)	State
Pruäf (m)	Occupation	sächzg	sixty	Schtadt (f)	Town
Pschtekk (n)	Cutlery	Saft (m)	Juice	Schtadt(f)	City
pschtelä	order (verb)	Salami (m)	Salami	Schtadtplan (m)	City map
Pschtellig (f)	Purchase order	Salär (n)	Salary	Schtägä (f)	Stairs
psezt	engaged	Salat (m)	Salad	Schtaibokk (m)	European ibex
Psizzer/in (m/f)	Owner	Salatsossä (f)	Dressing	Schtangä (f)	Draft beer
Pult (n)	Desk	Sali	Hi (informal)	schtarrä	stare (verb)
Punsch (m)	Punch	Salü	Hi (informal)	Schtazion(f)	Ward
Pürli (n)	Roll	salzig	salty	Schtekker (m)	Plug
Purscht (m)	young man	sammlä	collect (verb)	Schtiär (m)	Bull
Puzzma/frau (m/f)	Cleaner	Samschtig	Saturday	Schtirn (f)	Forehead
		sändä	send (verb)	Schträäl (m)	Comb
Q		Sandwich (m)	Sandwich	Schtrand (m)	Beach
		(Sändwitsch)		Schtrass (f)	Street
Quali(fikation) (f)	Appraisal	Satellit (m)	Satellite	Schtriit (m)	Argument
Quark (m)	Curd cheese	Satellitäschüsslä (f)	Satellite Dish	schtriitä	argue (verb)
		Sau (f)	Pig	Schtrümpf (pl)	Stockings
R		Schachtlä (f)	Box	Schtuäl (m)	Chair
		Schad!	What a shame!	Schtubä (f)	Lounge
Raam (m)	Cream	Schal (m)	Scarf	Schtudio (n)	Studio
Rächnig (f)	Invoice	Schalä (f)	Coffee with milk	Schtund (f)	Hour
rächts	right	Schalter (m)	Counter	Schtürä (pl)	Taxes
Radar (m)	Speed camera	Schampoo (n)	Shampoo	Schturm (m)	Storm
Radio (m)	Radio	scharf	spicy	Schuä (pl)	Shoes
Räge (m)	Rain	Schegg (m)	Cheque	Schuäl (f)	School
Rappä (m)	Rappen	schikkä	send (verb)	Schubladä (f)	Drawer
Rasä (m)	Lawn	Schildchrot (f)	Turtle	schüch	shy
Rasämäier (m)	Lawnmower	Schinkä (m)	Ham	Schulterä (f)	Shoulder
Raschtplazz (m)	Service area	schlächt	bad	Schüsslä (f)	Bowl
Raschtschtettä (f)	Service area	Schlaflosikait (f)	Insomnia	schüttlä	shake (verb)
Rasiärklingä (f)	Razor blades	Schlafzimmer (n)	Bedroom	Schwager (m)	Brother-in-law
Rauchereggä (m)	Smoking area	Schlagzilä (pl)	Headlines	Schwaineflaisch (n)	Pork
redä	speak (verb)	Schlangä (f)	Snake	schwarz	black
reduziert	Discount	schlapp	sleepy	Schwigermuetter (f)	Mother-in-law
Ree (n)	Roe deer	schlöfrig	sleepy	Schwigersoon (m)	Son-in-law
Reschtorant (m)	Restaurant	Schlüssel (m)	Key	Schwigertochter (f)	Daughter-in-law
reserviertä	reserve (verb)	Schmärzä (pl)	Pain	Schwigervatter (m)	Father -in-law
Rezäpt (n)	Prescription	schmärzhaft	painful	Schwiizer Frankä (m)	Swiss Francs
Rezepzion (f)	Reception	Schminkzüg (n)	Make-up	schwingä	Swiss wrestling
Resepzionischt/in (m/f)	Receptionist	Schmärzmittel (n)	Pain Killer	Schwinigs (n)	Pork
Riis (m)	Rice	schmökkä	smell	Schwö(schter) (f)	Sister
Riisecrevettä (f)	Prawns	schnäll	hurry	Schwögerin (f)	Sister-in-law
(Riisägröwettä)		Schnaps (m)	Spirit	schwul	gay
Rindflaisch (n)	Beef	Schnee (m)	Snow	schwümä	to swim
Rokk (m)	Skirt	Schnugi	sweetie	Schwümmbad (n)	Swimming pool
roo	raw	schön	beautiful	See (m)	Lake
rosa	pink	Schpäkk (m)	Bacon	Sekretär/in (m/f)	Secretary
Ross (n)	Horse	schparä	save (verb)	Sekundä (f)	second
rot	red	Schparkonto (n)	Savings account	sentimental	sentimental
Rotwii (m)	Red wine	schpaat	late	Septämber (m)	September
Rotä (m)	Red wine	Schpiägel (m)	Mirror	Serviettä (f)	Napkin
Rüäbli (n)	Carrots	Schpiil (n)	Game	sexy	sexy
Ruggä (m)	Back	Schpiiswagä (m)	Dining car	Shorts (pl)	Shorts

sibä	seven	Temperatur (f)	Temperature	Unggle (m)	Uncle
sibät	seventh	Tennisschuä (pl)	Tennis Shoes	Unglükkszaal (f)	unlucky number
sibäzg	seventy	Teppich (m)	Carpet	ungradi Zaalä	odd numbers
sich tränä	separate (verb)	Termin (m)	Appointment	Uniform (f)	Uniform
Sicherhait (f)	Security	Terrassä (f)	Terrace	under	beneath (prep)
Sidä (f)	Silk	Theater (n)	Theatre	under	under (prep)
sibzä	seventeen	Thema (n)	Subject	Undergschoss (n)	Basement
silber	silver (colour)	Tiger (m)	Tiger	Unterhaltig (f)	Entertainment
single	single	Tisch (m)	Table	Underhosä (f)	Panties
Sizzig (f)	Meeting	Tischmattä (f)	Table mats	Unterschrift (f)	Signature
Schnägg (m)	Slug	Tischset (n)	Dinner service	unzwungä	Business casual
SMS (n) (Äsämäs)	Text message	Tischtuäch (n)	Table cloth	Urgrosmuetter (f)	Great grandmother
so so (la la)	so-so	Tochter (f)	Daughter	Urgrosvatter (m)	Great grandfather
Soiffä (f)	Soap	Todesaazaig (f)	Obituary	us	from (prep)
Sokkä (pl)	Socks	Toilettä (f) (Tualettä)	Toilet	Ussländer/in (m/f)	Foreigner
Soon (m)	Son	Tollwuät (f)	Rabies	Ussland-Nachrichtä (pl)	International news
sorry	sorry	Tomatä (f)	Tomato	uufgreggt	excited
Steak (n) (Steik)	Steak	Tooscht (m)	Toast	Uuftrag (m)	Purchase order
süäss	sweet	trännt	separated	uusloggä	log out (verb)
Süässmoscht (m)	Apple juice	Tratsch (m)	Gossip	uuströchnä	dry out (verb)
sugä	suck (verb)	Traveller cheques(pl)	Travellers'cheque	uusgä	spend (verb)
Summer (m)	Summer	(Träwälär Schegg)		uusraisä	emigrate (verb)
Sunä (f)	Sun	trochä	dry	Uus-schtellig (f)	Exposition
Sunätach (n)	Sunshade	Ton (m)	Tuna	uus-tschäggä	check out (verb)
sunig	sunny	Tröpfli (pl)	Drops	Uusverchauff	Sale (rebate)
Sunntig	Sunday	Truthaan (m)	Turkey	uusziä	move out (verb)
Supermärt (m)	Supermarket	Truubesaft (m)	Grape juice		
suur	sour	truurig	sad	V	
suurä Moscht (m)	Cider	Tschüss	Bye (informal)		
Synagogä (f)	Synagogue	tschutä	play football(verb)	Vagina (f)	Vagina
		T-Shirt (n)	T-Shirt	Vatter (m)	Father
T		Tuäch (n)	Scarf	vegan(isch)	vegan
		Tüächli (n)	Towel	vegetarisch	vegetarian
Taal (n)	Valley	Tüfchüäler (m)	Freezer	Verband (m)	Bandage
Tach (n)	Roof	Tüfgarasch (f)	Basement garage	Verbilligung (f)	Discounts
Tachrinnä (f)	Gutters	tüfgfrorä	frozen	Verbindig (f)	Connection
Tachwonig (f)	Attic flat	Tumbler (m)	Tumble drier	verbränä	burn (verb)
Tag (m)	Day	(Tömbler)		Verchoiffer/in (m/f)	Salesperson
Taigwarä (pl)	Pasta	Turi (m) (slang)	Tourist	verchauffä	sell (verb)
Tail (m)	Section	Turischt/in (m/f)	Tourist	Vercheltig (f)	Cold
tailziit	Part time	tüür	expensive	vergangä	past
Take away (m)	Take away	Tüür (f)	Door	Vergangähait (f)	Past
(Teik Awei)		tuusig	thousand	vergiftet	poisoned
Talk Show (f)	Talk show			Verhüetigsmittel (n)	Contraceptive
(Tok Schou)		U		verhüratet	married
Täller (m)	Plate			Verlezzig (f)	Injury
Talliä (f)	Waist	über	above (prep)	verlobt	engaged
Tankschtell (f)	Petrol station	über	across (prep)	Verlobtä (m)	Fiancé
Tantä (f)	Aunt	über	over (prep)	Verlobti (f)	Fiancée
tanzä	dance (verb)	überrascht	surprised	Verluscht (m)	Loss
Tassä (f)	Cup	Überschtundä (pl)	Overtime	Vermieter/in (m/f)	Landlord
Täschä (f)	Bag	überwiisä	transfer (verb)	Vermittlig (f)	Operator
Techniker/in (m/f)	Technician	uf	on (horiz.surface)	verrukkt	crazy
Tee (m)	Tea		(prep)	Verschpötig (f)	Delay
Teelöffeli (n)	Teaspoon	Uf widerluägä	Bye	Versicherig (f)	Insurance
Teeni (m) (Tiini)	Teenager	Uf widersee!	Bye	Versicherigsnummerä(f)	Insurance number
Telefonbeantworter (m)	Answering machine	ufä	up	Vertailer (m)	Digestive
		Ufenthaltsgenemigung(f)	Residence permit	Vertrag (m)	Contract
Telefonbuäch (n)	Telephone book	um	around (prep)	Verwaltig (f)	Estate agency
Telefonchartä (f)	Telephone card	umarmä	hug (verb)	Verwaltigsrat (m)	Board of Directors
Telefonnummerä (f)	Phone number	und	plus (maths)	Verwandti (pl)	Relatives
Telefonrächnig (f)	Telephone bill	Underwösch (f)	Underwear	verwitwet	widowed

verzollä	declare (verb)	Wimperä (pl)	Eyelash
verzwiiflet	desperate	Wind (m)	Wind
vier	four	Wind sörfä	Wind surfing
viert	fourth	Windä (f)	Attic
vierzä	fourteen	Winter (m)	Winter
vierzg	forty	Wirus (m)	Virus
vill	many	wiiss	white
vill	much	Wiissbrot (n)	White bread
violett	violet	Wiisswii (m)	White wine
VIP (m) (Wiaipi)	Celebrity	Wiissä (m)	White wine
vo	from (prep)	Wisum (n)	Visa
vo	of (prep)	Witwe (f)	Widow
Vogel (m)	Bird	Witwer (m)	Widower
Vollkornbrot (n)	Whole grain bread	Wizz (m)	Joke
Vollpension (f)	Full board	wizzig	funny
vollziit	Full time	Wo?	Where?
vor	in front of (prep)	Wohi?	Where to?
Vorhallä (f)	Lobby	Wolf (m)	Wolf
Vorhäng (pl)	Curtains	wolkig	cloudy
Vorruum (m)	Lobby	Wösch (f)	Laundry
Vorschpiis (f)	Starter	Wöschchuchi (f)	Laundry room
Vorwaal (f)	Area code	Wöschmaschine (f)	Washing machine
		Wöschmittel (n)	Detergent
W		Wöschplan (m)	Laundry schedule
		Wöschsakk (m)	Laundry bag
Waag (f)	Scales	Wöschtag (m)	Laundry day
Wäärig (f)	Currency	Wuchä (f)	Week
Wächselratä (f)	Exchange rate	Wuchänänd (n)	Weekend
Wäg (m)	Footpath	Wulä (f)	Wool
Wäg (m)	Path	Wurm (m)	Worm
Wäjä (f)	Pie	Wurscht (f)	Sausage
Wald (m)	Forest		
Wält (f)	World	**Z**	
Wänn?	When?		
Wanzä (f)	Bug	zä	ten
Wär?	Who?	Zaa (m)	Tooth
Warähuus (n)	Warehouse	Zaabürschteli (n)	Toothbrush
Wärbig (f)	Advertising	Zaapaschtä (f)	Toothpaste
warm	warm	zät	tenth
Warum?	Why?	Zaine (f)	Laundry basket
Was ?	What ?	Zäjä (m)	Toe
wäschä	wash (verb)	Zäjänagel (m)	Toenail
Wäschpi (n)	Wasp	zalä	pay (verb)
Wasser mit Cholesüüri	Water with gas	Zalig (f)	Payment
Wasser ooni Cholesüüri	Water without gas	Zältli (n)	Candy
Wassermelonä (f)	Watermelon	Zander (m)	Jack salmon
Wätter (m)	Weather	zaubärä	magic, to do (verb)
Wätterpricht (m)	Forecast	Zauberai (f)	Magic
Wätterpricht (m)	Weather report	Zebra (n)	Zebra
WC (n) (Weze)	Toilet	zfridä	joyful
WC-Papier (n)	Toilet paper	Ziischtig	Tuesday
(Weze-Papier)		Zimmer (n)	Room
Wekkaaruäf (m)	Wake up call	Zimmerservice(m)	Room service
wenig	few	(Zimmer-Serwis)	
weniger	less	Zins (m)	Interest
Wiä?	How?	Zitig (f)	Newspaper
Wii (m)	Wine	Zitrone (f)	Lemon
wiit	wide	Zmittag (m)	Lunch
wiiterlaitä	forward (verb)	Zmittagässä (n)	Lunch
wiitsichtig	long-sighted	Zmorgä (m)	Breakfast
Wildsau (f)	Wild boar	Znacht (m)	Dinner
Willkomä	Welcome		

Znachtassä (n)	Dinner
Znüni (m)	Snack (morning)
Zoll (m)	Customs
Zoo (m)	Zoo
zruggschriibä	reply (verb)
zu	to (prep)
zuähebä	cover (verb)
Zuäkumft (f)	Future
zuäkümftig	Future
Zug (m)	Train
Zugbilet (n)	Train ticket
zuhandä vo	Care of
Zukker (m)	Sugar
Zungä (f)	Tongue
Zvieri (m)	Snack (afternoon)
zwai	two
zwaihundert	two hundred
zwait	second
zwaituusig	two thousand
Zwaizimmerwonig (f)	Two-room apt.
zwänzg	twenty
Zwiblä (f)	Onion
Zwilling (pl)	Twins
zwinkerä	wink (verb)
zwölf	twelve
zwüschä	between (prep)

THE END (DÄ SCHLUSS)

Index

A

Age 93
Agencies 98–101
Alcohol 49
Alemannic 6
Animals 108–109
Apartment. *See* Flat
Articles 128
 Definite Articles 128
 Indefinite Articles 128
Asking questions 24

B

Banking. *See* Money
Bread 52
Bugs. *See* Insects

C

Clothing 70–71
Clothing materials 71
Coffee 48
Colours 107
 Colour expressions 107
Communication 38–45
Customs. *See* Immigration

D

Days of the Week 112
Dialektgemisch 5
Dairy Products 52
Diets 52
Diglossia 8
Directions 77–79

 Reference Points 78
Dress Code 36
Drinks 48–49

E

Entertainment 86–89
E-mail 40–41
Emergency 64
Emotions 61–63
Estate Agent 100. *See also* Landlord
Exchange Office 73. *See also* Money

F

Family 90–92
Flat 98
Flavours 50
Food 46–47, 50–53
 Places to Eat 53
 Shopping 52
Formal 20
Fruit 52

G

General Non-Specific Terms 106
 Generic Measures 106
 Generic Quantity 106
 Generic Time 106
 Generic Words 106
Geography 82
Greetings 20–23
 Hello (Formal) 20
 Hello (Informal) 21
 Politeness 23

H

Health 54–57
Health Problems 57
Health Remedies 57
High German in Switzerland 8–11
History of the Dialects 6–7
Hospital 56
Hotels 80–81
Parts of the House 95
Housing 94–101
The Human Body 58–59
  Body Activities 60

I

Idioms 122–125. *See also* Colour
  expressions
Immigration 66
Informal 20–21
Insects 109
Introducing Yourself 25
Invitations 28

J

Job Title 37

K

Kitchen 96

L

Landlord 99–101. *See* also Estate
  Agent
Laundry 99
Legumes 50
Love 29–32
  Loveless 32

M

Meals 47
Measurements 47
Meat 47
Midlands 4–5
Misfortune 33
Money 72–73
Months of the Year 112
Mountains (Terms) 84

N

Neighbours 98–101
News 44–45
Numbers 102–103
  Cardinal Numbers 103
  Ordinal Numbers 102

O

Outdoors 82–85

P

Paperwork 34
Payment 36. *See also* Money
Permits for foreigners 66
Pet names 29
Phonetics 18–19
  Consonants 18
  Vowels 19
Police 65
Postal offers 43
Pronouns 128–129
  Demonstrative Pronouns 129
  Personal Pronouns 128
  Possessive Pronouns 129

R

Relatives. *See* Family
Röschtigraben 12

S

Safety. *See* Emergency and Police
Seafood 50
Seasons 110
Secondos 13–14
Sexual Preferences 30
Sharing the bill 53
Shopping 68–69
Slang 118–121
Small Talk 25–27
  First Approach 27
  Getting Personal 26
  Negative Answers 27
SMS 41
Snow (Terms) 83–84
Socializing. *See* Greetings
Special Moments 33
Swiss Dishes 51
Swiss Drinks 49
Swiss Traditions 89
Swiss Events 28
Sympathy 33

T

Telephoning 38–39
Temperature. *See* Weather
Time 110–113
  Moments in Time 111
  Parts of the Day 110
  Telling Time 113
  Time Measurements 110
Time at Work 36

Toiletries 97
Toilets 104–105
Transportation 74–76
  Special ticket offers 75
  Ticket Controller 75
Traveling 74–89

U

Upper German 6

V

Vegetables 50
Verbs 130–131
  Modal Verbs 131
  Verb Endings 131

W

Weather 114–115
Wedding Stuff 31
Wildlife 108
Work 34–37
Working Areas 36

About the Authors...

Sergio J. Lievano is an Anglo-Colombian artist brought up in the surroundings of the fresh, natural environment of his family's 'Hacienda', a coffee plantation high up in the Andes.

Sergio is a qualified Economist from Los Andes University in Colombia, and worked for more than 12 years in several countries as a Business Advisor and Project Manager. Much of this experience was in the Fragrance industry. He also studied Comics and Illustrations at the Joso Comic School in Barcelona, where he developed his cartoonist talent.

Sergio has written two other books…but he still cannot remember in which computer file he saved them...

Currently he is focusing on his writing, cartoons and illustrations, and resides in Switzerland…in the Swiss German speaking part.

N icole Egger was born and grew up in Zurich. She received her master's in linguistics and literature from the University of Zurich. During her studies and since her degree she has been teaching German and Swiss German to the increasingly international community in Switzerland.

She spent a year in Beijing learning Chinese which enables her to sympathise with newcomers to Switzerland who are confronted with a difficult, funny-sounding language. Since she has a strong interest in understanding the mechanisms of different languages and has also studied Latin, English, French, Spanish and Portuguese, she is perceptive to the difficulties that students may encounter. But her real challenge is to encourage people who are learning a foreign language to become confident and competent in a way that they can have fun doing it.

Acknowledgements

Many people have helped in many ways to make this book a reality. They have given us their time and knowledge to help this book be amusing and useful. To all of them our sincere gratitude. In particular we would like to mention:

Dianne Dicks, Angela Joos, Ruth Loynes de Lievano, Anja Kauf, Claudia Holenstein, Michael Landolt, Roberto Lievano, Miguel Lievano, Jürg and Britta Jacob, Manuel Kauf, Marcel Untersander, Ingrid Larsen, Hsiang–Yun Tseng, André Klauser and David Pybus.

About Bergli Books

Bergli Books publishes, promotes and distributes books in English that focus on travel, on living in Switzerland and on intercultural matters:

Ticking Along with the Swiss, edited by Dianne Dicks, entertaining and informative personal experiences of many 'foreigners' living in Switzerland. ISBN 978-3-9520002-4-3.

Ticking Along Too, edited by Dianne Dicks, has more personal experiences, a mix of social commentary, warm admiration and observations of the Swiss as friends, neighbours and business partners. ISBN 978-3-9520002-1-2.

Ticking Along Free, edited by Dianne Dicks, with more stories about living with the Swiss, this time with also some prominent Swiss writers. ISBN 978-3-905252-02-6.

Ticking Along on Tape, a 60-minute audio cassette with a selection of ten readings from Ticking Along with the Swiss and Ticking Along Too. ISBN 978-3-905252-00-2.

Cupid's Wild Arrows; intercultural romance and its consequences, edited by Dianne Dicks, contains personal experiences of 55 authors living with two worlds in one partnership. ISBN 978-3-9520002-2-9.

Laughing Along with the Swiss, by Paul Bilton has everything you need to know to endear you to the Swiss forever. ISBN 978-3-905252-01-9.

A Taste of Switzerland, by Sue Style, with over 50 recipes that show the richness of this country's diverse gastronomic cultures. ISBN 978-3-9520002-7-4.

The Surprising Wines of Switzerland, a practical guide to Switzerland's best kept secret, by John C. Sloan, an objective and comprehensive description of Swiss wines. ISBN 978-3-9520002-6-7.

Inside Outlandish, by Susan Tuttle, illustrated by ANNA, a collection of essays that takes you to the heart of feeling at home in strange, new places. ISBN 978-3-9520002-8-1.

Berne; a portrait of Switzerland's federal capital, of its people, culture and spirit, by Peter Studer (photographs), Walter Däpp, Bernhard Giger and Peter Krebs. ISBN 978-3-9520002-9-8.

Red Benches and others; a journal/notebook for your viewpoints, with photography of benches throughout Switzerland by Clive Minnitt and Frimmel Smith and blank pages for your notes. ISBN 978-3-905252-08-8.

Once Upon an Alp, by Eugene V. Epstein. A selection of the best stories from this well-known American/Swiss humorist. ISBN 978-3-905252-05-7.

Lifting the Mask – your guide to Basel Fasnacht, by Peter Habicht, illustrations by Fredy Prack. ISBN 978-3-905252-04-0.

pfyffe ruesse schränze – eine Einführung in die Basler Fasnacht, von Peter Habicht, Illustrationen von Fredy Prack. (German edition of Lifting the Mask.) ISBN 978-3-905252-09-5.

Beyond Chocolate – understanding Swiss culture, by Margaret Oertig-Davidson, an in-depth discussion of the cultural attitudes and values of the Swiss for newcomers and long-term residents. ISBN 978-3-905252-06-4.

Schokolade ist nicht alles – ein Leitfaden zur Schweizer Kultur, von Margaret Oertig-Davidson. Ein Führer durch die Schweizer Lebensart für jeden Neuankömmling und alle, die sich bereits als Insider fühlen. (German edition of Beyond Chocolate.) ISBN 978-3-905252-10-1.

Culture Smart! Switzerland, by Kendall Maycock. A quick guide to customs, etiquette and history of Switzerland. ISBN 978-3-905252-12-5.

Swiss Me, by Roger Bonner, illustrations by Edi Barth. Humorous stories about life in Switzerland. ISBN 978-3-905252-11-8.

Hoi Zäme – Schweizerdeutsch leicht gemacht, von Sergio J. Lievano und Nicole Egger. (German edition of Hoi – your Swiss German survival guide). ISBN 978-3-905252-14-9.

Hoi! Et après... – manuel de survie en suisse allemand, by Sergio J. Lievano and Nicole Egger. (French edition of Hoi – your Swiss German survival guide). ISBN 978-3-905252-16-3.

Ticking Along with Swiss Kids, by Dianne Dicks and Katalin Fekete, illustrations by Marc Locatelli. A colourful and fun way for children from ages 6 to 12 to learn all they need to enjoy making friends and feeling at home, about Swiss languages, food, festivities, what kids read, sing, play and how they get along. Includes songs with their musical scores, a one-act play, maps, lists of places to visit and a 32-card language game, photographs and playful cartoons and illustrations throughout. ISBN 978-3-905252-15-6.

Swiss Cookies – biscuits for Christmas and all year round, by Andrew Rushton and Katalin Fekete, a selection of the most famous and traditional Swiss cookies and bakes, with photographs, a guide to ingredients and measurement conversions. ISBN 978-3-905252-17-0.

Ask for a catalogue or visit

www.bergli.ch

Dear Reader,

Your opinion can help us. We would like to know what you think of *Hoi – your Swiss German survival guide*.

Where did you learn about this book?

Had you heard about Bergli Books before reading this book?

What did you enjoy about this book?

Any criticism?

Would you like to receive more information about the books we publish and distribute? If so, please give us your name and address and we'll send you a catalogue.

Name:

Address:

City/Country:

Bergli Books
Rümelinsplatz 19
CH-4001 Basel
Switzerland